Getting Out of Debt and Staying Out

Getting Out of Debt and Staying Out

Face up to financial reality
and free yourself from money
worries...

Tony Palmer

First published in 2005 by
How To Books Ltd,
3 Newtec Place, Magdalen Road,
Oxford OX4 1RE. United Kingdom.
Tel: (01865) 793806. Fax: (01865) 248780.
email: info@howtobooks.co.uk
http://www.howtobooks.co.uk

British Library Cataloguing in Publication Data
A catalogue record for this book is available from the British
Library

Cover design by Baseline Arts Ltd, Oxford
Produced for How To Books by Deer Park Productions, Tavistock
Typeset by PDQ Typesetting, Newcastle-under-Lyme, Staffs
Printed and bound by Cromwell Press, Trowbridge, Wiltshire

NOTE: The material contained in this book is set out in good
faith for general guidance and no liability can be accepted
for loss or expense incurred as a result of relying in particular
circumstances on statements made in the book. The laws and
regulations are complex and liable to change, and readers should
check the current position with the relevant authorities before
making personal arrangements.

Contents

Introduction

nodern life. Just
or another: a
balance, a car
types. The easy
ely recent thing.
iard to come by,
ntrolled by the
ied' by building

hing Victorians

disapproved of more than sex t. 'Debt' has an
unpleasant ring to it, particularly to the older generation.
It's also a lot less fun than sex.

But like sex, we can't do without it. We need to know how
to handle it, so that we control *it*, rather than it controlling
us.

What is really important is:

♦ to understand what we are doing when we go into debt

♦ to know how much it is actually costing us

- to ensure we have shopped around to keep that cost to the minimum

- to be sure we can afford what it costs – even if our circumstances change

- to have a plan to pay off the debt at a realistic time in the future.

In this book, we look at how people have got into trouble with debt, mainly due to changing circumstances. We work out what action they could take to get out of the mess.

We then look in much greater detail at how to borrow in a way which will minimise the risk of getting into difficulties, and how to do it at the lowest cost.

Finally, if the worst happens and you do get into a financial mess, we look at how you can get out of it with the least long-term damage.

Our Case Studies

In this chapter we meet a variety of people who have got into debt. They weren't stupid or, except in one case, irresponsible. Their problems arose because circumstances changed. Their circumstances and other people's. Some changes could have been foreseen, others not. They were things that can and do happen to anybody at any time.

We also see how, in two of the cases, it was possible with a lot of thought and discussion, and a bit of helpful advice, to get out of the mess they were in. One case relates the sad tale of what happens if you don't take the right action at the right time to get matters straight.

JANET AND JOHN

An everyday story of professional folk hit by rising interest rates and one or two other problems.

It is 2007. Janet and John are in their late thirties. They set up home together in Sheffield in a rented flat in 2002 and decided to get married and buy a house in 2003. John is a software engineer and in 2003 was earning £30,000. Janet is a qualified nurse who was earning £20,000 p.a. When they bought the house they had £20,000 savings.

They found a three bedroomed house they liked in the suburbs of Sheffield for £155,000 and, as first time buyers outside a chain, had their offer of £150,000 accepted. They had no difficulty in getting an offer of a mortgage of £135,000 (2.7 times income). In fact, the building society persuaded them to take a 95% mortgage (£142,500) and told them there would have been no problem in getting a mortgage of four times joint income if they had chosen a more expensive house.

Janet and John were cautious. They didn't want to over-extend themselves. They were planning to start a family and were aware that Janet's income might go down if she decided she needed to work part-time for a period while the children were young. They also knew they were going to have to spend about £10,000 on a new kitchen and bathroom for the house, which had been lived in by an elderly couple and needed a fair bit of modernisation. The 95% mortgage would enable them to do this without making big inroads into their savings. They needed £7,500 of their savings to meet the gap between the mortgage offered and the purchase price, and another £1,000 to cover legal and survey costs.

The survey report required by the building society had referred to the condition of the roof and the lender had put a condition on the mortgage that minor repairs should be carried out to the roof and gutters within 12 months. They agreed to this and the £142,500 25-year repayment mortgage was finalised. They decided on a variable interest rate mortgage at 4.5% because the fixed rate and capped rates meant a slightly higher monthly payment. They paid £792 per month which covered both interest and capital repayment.

August 2003

Janet and John moved in to their first real home in August 2003, and immediately set about redecorating and improving the house, and having a new kitchen and bathroom installed. These improvements inevitably cost them more than they expected (£12,000 rather than the £10,000 they had budgeted for) and they were pleased that they had agreed to take out the larger mortgage. Their savings were used up – but they expected to be able to bring them up to a safe level again out of their current earnings, which gave them a reasonable margin above their living costs.

In December 2003 the Bank of England raised the Minimum Lending Rate by 0.25% and their variable rate mortgage rose by 0.25%. Their monthly payments increased to £812. Then in February 2004 the Bank of England raised their rates by another 0.25% to 4% and again their mortgage rate increased by 0.25%. Their monthly payments rose to £833.

They were not greatly worried by these increases. The papers had all been saying that interest rates were bound to go up sooner or later. After all, interest rates in 2003 had been at their lowest levels for nearly 50 years. Janet told John that she was pleased they had not gone for a more expensive house with a larger mortgage even though the building society would have been willing to give them one.

March 2004

In March 2004 John's company won a big contract to install software in offices in Bristol. It would mean quite a bit of overtime for three months, although it would involve him being away during the week. At about this time, Janet's old P registered car had started playing up. They didn't want to risk it breaking down while John was away and decided to get her a new, or rather, nearly new car. Their savings were still only a few hundred pounds so they took out a five-year personal loan of £8,000 at 9% from their bank, costing £166 per month.

April 2004

At about the same time, the couple realised that they had better do something about getting the roof repaired in order to have it completed within a year of getting the mortgage. They started looking for a reliable builder to give them a quote for the repairs. In April 2004 Sheffield was hit by a very severe spring gale which caused structural damage all over the city. Their house was in a particularly exposed position near the top of one of the hills which surround the city centre. Their already suspect roof was badly damaged, with slates and the underfelt being ripped off. There was also quite bad damage caused to their neighbours' car by flying slates.

Their insurance company helped them find a builder who put an emergency tarpaulin over the roof, but it became clear that a completely new roof and new guttering were going to be required. Never mind, they thought, we are fully insured. There will be a lot of inconvenience but they would only have a £200 excess to pay on the insurance claim.

Their neighbour was understanding about the damage to his car, which was estimated at about £3,000. Naturally he didn't want to claim on his car insurance and risk his no claims bonus and have to pay an excess. It was agreed that he would claim against Janet and John's house insurer.

Then a problem arose. As the policy had been taken out so recently, the insurer asked to see the surveyor's report on the house. When they saw the report on the condition of the roof and the fact that the recommended repairs had not been carried out, they refused to meet the claim. Janet and John were devastated. The total repair bill, including their neighbour's car repair, was going to come to about £15,000. After many letters and phone calls, during which work on the roof stopped and the tarpaulin let quite a bit of water into their new bathroom, the insurer agreed to meet 50% of the total bill.

" Not our problem. "

This was a problem, but not a disaster. They went to their building society who were sympathetic. They accepted that Janet and John had intended to carry out the roof repairs within the 12 months stipulated in the mortgage offer. They could see that their incomes were secure and that the necessary repairs were being done.

In the nine months since Janet and John had moved in, the house had risen in value by 10% to £165,000. There was scope, therefore, to increase the mortgage, without the outstanding mortgage going above 95% of the house's value. They had to pay for a valuation and some legal fees (£250) but within weeks of going to the building society they had a cheque for £10,000. The monthly payments on the mortgage rose to £891, but there was £2,500 left over from their share of the roof and car repairs for their emergency savings fund, which they had begun to realise was vital.

During the summer there were three further rises of 0.25% each in the Bank of England Minimum Lending Rate. The building society put the mortgage rate up by the same amount each time. By December 2004 they were paying a mortgage rate of 5.75%, meaning monthly payments of £959.

December 2004
By December 2004, Janet was four months pregnant. They were delighted. Yes, things were going to be a bit tight financially, what with the rise in interest rates and the extra borrowing. But it was nothing to worry about. Although John's overtime in Bristol had only lasted a few weeks earlier in the year, he had had a rise in his basic

salary of nearly 5% since they took on the mortgage and was now earning £31,500.

The plan was that Janet would stop work in mid April, about six weeks before the baby was due in late May/early June. She wanted to take at least nine months off work after the baby was born and then go back to work full time. Her mother, who lived close to them, would look after the baby during her working hours. If she found that full-time working was too much, she would reduce her hours. The NHS had family friendly policies and was desperate to keep qualified nurses for however many hours they were prepared to work.

In the winter of 2004/5, the Minimum Lending Rate went up by another 0.25% to 5% and their mortgage rate to 6.0%. Their monthly mortgage payment was now £982.

June 2005
The baby arrived on 3 June 2005 and was beautiful. They called her June and joyfully accepted that their lives and lifestyle had changed forever.

Janet got maternity pay for 26 weeks, and when that stopped they started to transfer £500 per month from their savings into their current account to pay the part of the monthly mortgage direct debit which they couldn't manage on John's salary alone. By the end of the year though, things were getting tight. Savings were down from the £2,000 they started with to zero, even allowing for the extra £2,500 they had remaining from the increased borrowing of £10,000 from the building society.

Janet decided she needed to go back to work immediately after Christmas, a little earlier than she had originally planned. She agreed with the hospital where she worked that she would initially do 20 hours a week and go back full time in March.

January 2006

During January 2006, while they were waiting for her first pay cheque at the end of the month, they decided to make the minimum payment on their credit card. Up until then they had always paid off their credit card bill in full, knowing that the interest rate they paid on the outstanding amount would be around 12% – nearly double what they paid on their mortgage. They were confident they would be able to pay off the full amount again in February. Unfortunately, the January credit card bill had been a heavy one, with Christmas spending – particularly presents for June's first Christmas. When February came round they decided they could only pay off half, but were confident they could pay off in full in March. In April everything would be fine, as Janet would be back at work full time.

May 2006

Then disaster struck. And this time it was a disaster, and totally unforeseen. Janet's mother had found looking after June very tiring. Hardly surprising as she was in her early sixties. She began to get out of breath and have minor chest pains when she was keeping up with June after she started crawling. She went to the doctor, who diagnosed mild angina. Nothing too serious, he said, prescribing pills. But he also said she really must give up looking after June, at least for the time being.

This faced Janet and John with a dilemma. Janet had to keep on working if they were to keep out of financial problems. But who was going to look after June? There was a crèche at the hospital, but there was a waiting list for places. They said they might be able to squeeze her in for a couple of mornings in about three months' time when one of the other children went to nursery school, but that was all they could offer. There was nothing for it but to find some private childcare.

This they did, but at a cost. In fact, it cost £70 about half of Jane's net pay. They realised, a the more hours she worked, the more it woul would in effect, if she worked full time, hav money after paying for child care as if she working 20 hours a week. They would only ju heads above water at that rate.

In fact, with the extra costs of the bab travelling to the child minder (in another par they found it necessary to put more on their credit card. By the end of June 2006, the outstanding balance on the credit card was £3,000 – an extra £30 per month was being added in interest charges alone.

Janet and John's action plan
Janet and John are an intelligent and responsible couple. They realised that they were now spending more than they were earning and that this could not continue indefinitely. In fact, they realised that the sooner they did something about their situation, the better.

Reducing the balance on their credit card

The main source of their worry was the growing outstanding balance on the credit card. They recognised that it was ridiculous to pay a rate of interest which was double the rate they were paying on their mortgage. The answer, they thought, lay in borrowing more – say another £10,000 on their mortgage. This would enable them to pay off the credit card debt and establish a cash reserve for the difficult months ahead. After all, Janet told John, they should get June into the crèche full time eventually and that was much, much cheaper than the private child minder. They would have to put off having the second baby for two or three years until John got promotion or a higher paid job – but that was not the end of the world.

So they went to see their building society manager. He was sympathetic, but this time there was a problem. Since they had increased their mortgage, house prices had stopped rising. In fact, in their particular area, where jobs were increasingly hard to come by, house prices had actually started to fall. They weren't in a 'negative equity' situation yet – but there was no spare equity in the property on which a larger loan could be given.

They tried three or four other lenders. The story was the same with most of them. One offered them a bigger mortgage, but the rate of interest was higher than they were paying on the existing mortgage, with a lot of up front fees and charges. They felt that would only add to their problems.

They sat down to talk things through. They realised they could get a personal loan of £3,000 from their own bank at an interest rate of 11% APR – more than a mortgage, but less than the credit card interest. It wouldn't help them with a reserve, but it would enable them to pay off the credit card. It would cost (including capital repayments) £65 per month. Their anxiety about the escalating credit card debt was such that they decided to go for it and signed up.

October 2006
The increases in interest rates of the last two years were not just affecting Janet and John. They were having an effect on the economy as a whole. Economic growth started to slow, house prices stabilised and unemployment started to rise slightly. Slightly maybe, but John's job was one of those affected. In October 2006 he was called into his boss's office and told that they were having to let some staff go as their customers had cut back on investment in computer hardware and software. They would prefer not to make him formally redundant, and would offer him three months' salary in lieu of notice if he voluntarily resigned. He realised that this was more than he would get in statutory redundancy pay and the one month's notice to which he was legally entitled. Also, it would be tax free. He decided to take the offer. After all, he and Janet had the mortgage protection insurance in case of illness or unemployment and the lump sum payment of the salary in lieu of notice would help with the cash flow, particularly if he got another job quickly.

Unfortunately, he didn't. Christmas came and went and that was inevitably expensive. After all, they couldn't let June miss out on Christmas because they had temporary problems.

January 2007

After Christmas, when the three months for which he had been paid expired, John went to the Job Centre. That was when he got his first shock. Because he had 'voluntarily' given up his job (which was how the Job Centre saw it), he was not entitled to Job Seekers' Allowance immediately. They were prepared, however, to pay his National Insurance Credits, which kept his contribution record complete for his pension.

The second and more serious blow was that when they claimed on the mortgage protection policy, they were refused. 'Look at the conditions' the insurance company told them. 'We only pay out in cases of compulsory redundancy. You gave up the job voluntarily.' Janet and John took advice, but they were told that this was happening all the time. Mortgage Protection Policies were one of those insurance deals that made insurance companies a lot of money because they rarely paid out. The small print contained a lot of exclusions.

Clearly Janet would have to go back to work full time, with John looking after June on the three days a week when she was not at the child minder's. The hospital was delighted to have her back full time.

Overview of Janet and John's situation

This was the situation in which our couple found themselves in early 2007. They had to find mortgage payments of £982 per month, payments on their personal loans of £231 per month, council tax was £110 per month and child minding cost £280 per month. Then they had to eat, keep the house warm and find the money for all the other necessities of daily living. In total, their outgoings were £2,320 per month and their net income from Janet's salary was £1,200 per month.

Janet and John were facing a crisis and they knew it. The situation had not come about because they had acted foolishly. In fact, they had been cautious in all their decisions. Perhaps their only mistakes had been to take out a variable rather than a fixed rate or capped mortgage, and not to read the small print on their mortgage protection policy. And those are mistakes which anyone could make. Rather, they had been the victims of circumstances – economic circumstances, family circumstances – even the weather. It can – and does – happen to anyone.

Did they add to their troubles by taking some unwise decisions? After all, we all make mistakes.

Before we look at how Janet and John got out of their difficulties – and be reassured that they did – let's look at what might have happened if they had been less cautious.

GARY AND SUE: HOW THINGS MIGHT HAVE BEEN WORSE

Let us imagine that Janet and John have alter egos – Gary and Sue. In 2003, Gary and Sue have identical circumstances to Janet and John – the same salaries and the same types of jobs. Sue even got pregnant at the same time as Janet.

While Janet and John took cautious, sensible decisions, Gary and Sue took some rash, unwise ones.

Even though they had very little in the way of savings they went for the most expensive house they could finance with the biggest mortgage offer they could get. This was a £200,000 house with a four times joint salary 95% mortgage. It took all their savings to fund the 5% deposit. They decided on an interest-only mortgage because the monthly outgoings would be less than a repayment mortgage. They believed that by the time they needed to repay the capital in 2033, house prices would have escalated so much that they could pay off what, by then, would seem a tiny sum by moving to a smaller, cheaper house. It could have been worse. Some of the less reputable financial institutions were offering self-certified income mortgages. On that basis, they could have got a mortgage of up to five times joint income. As it was, their monthly interest-only mortgage cost them £752 per month.

February 2004
When interest rates started rising, Gary and Sue took it in their stride. They didn't feel they needed to cut back at all even though the mortgage interest payments went up to £791 per month in February 2004. They let their credit cards take the strain. They were a bit surprised at the £10,000 credit limit they were each allowed on their separate credit cards, but if the banks were happy, who were they to quibble? They paid the minimum payment each month.

Their house didn't need a new kitchen, but they decided to have a new bathroom and the company that provided and fitted it for £6,000 were happy to be paid on Sue's credit card.

November 2004

Gary and Sue were lucky that their house, unlike Janet and John's, wasn't damaged in the April 2004 storm. However, when Sue became pregnant in November, they weren't as delighted as Janet and John as they had not been planning to have a baby for another two or three years, when they were confident Gary would have a promotion and a much bigger salary.

January 2005

The prospect of the baby made them look at their finances. They realised that their credit card bills were fairly daunting. Between them they had £15,000 outstanding and were paying £150 per month in interest charges alone. They decided that what they needed to do was to increase their mortgage to take advantage of the fact that the house had increased in value to £260,000 by January 2005, even though the big increases in house prices in 2003 and 2004 had begun to slow.

Gary felt his car needed replacing – it was, after all, four years old. If they raised another £25,000 on the mortgage, the repayments would only go up to £1,030 per month and they could use the money to pay off the credit card debt and buy a new car. That seemed to them a pretty shrewd financial deal: the mortgage was still only £215,000 on a house valued at £260,000.

July 2005

When interest rates went up again in July 2005 they had risen 1.5% since they first took out their mortgage. The minimum lending rate had gone from 3.5% in the summer of 2003 to 5% two years later. Mortgage rates had gone from 4.5% to 6.0%. 1.5% didn't sound a lot to Gary and Sue, but to their surprise, they found their monthly mortgage interest payments had risen from £712 per month when they took on the mortgage to £1,075 per month now (including the additional loan of £25,000). £363 per month was a big increase, even for middle class professionals like Gary and Sue in reasonably well paid jobs.

Of course, they were an intelligent couple and realised they would have to cut back now that Sue was going to be on maternity leave. She wouldn't be able to go back to work very quickly as they had no relatives living close by to help with childcare. In any case, when Robert arrived, Sue was so enchanted with him that she knew she couldn't leave him with a babyminder or in a crèche all day – even if she could find one at a reasonable cost. They would have to learn to live on Gary's income.

Unfortunately, a significant proportion of Gary's income had been in the form of performance bonuses. As the economy slackened off towards the end of 2005, the amount of work available reduced and so did his bonuses. His salary fell back towards his basic of £23,000.

They now had mortgage interest payments of £1,075 to meet out of a net monthly salary of £1,400. With their other living costs of at least £1,000 per month and the expenses of a new baby this was clearly going to be impossible. And so it proved.

At first they coped by buying essentials on their credit cards. This helped their cash flow, but they soon realised that the total credit outstanding was going up fast, along with the interest payment and the minimum payment due. Sue found a child minder and returned to work part time. Unfortunately, the child minder was on the other side of the city from where she worked. She hated leaving the baby with someone else, but she had little choice.

Even so the time and cost of getting to the babyminder in the morning and collecting him in the evening on the two days a week she worked made the working days totally exhausting. And after she had paid the taxi fares to do it (she had sold her car when she stopped working) plus the cost of the child minding, there didn't seem much money left from all that effort – certainly not enough to solve their financial problems.

The credit card bills got bigger. Then their bank wrote to them to say they had gone above their authorised overdraft. That one month's unauthorised overdraft of

£30 cost them £50 in charges and interest. The same thing happened the following month and the bank, after making the same charge again, agreed to give them an increased authorised overdraft facility of £250 at 16% p.a. interest. They started getting final demands for electricity, gas and telephone bills. The bank agreed to increase the overdraft to £1,000, but soon they were running up to that limit too. The bank said it could not increase the limit further.

January 2007
In January 2007 the bank refused to accept the direct debit on council tax. The following month the bank did the same for the mortgage interest. Gary and Sue did not know which way to turn.

They had to eat and heat the house and Gary had to have the car to get to work. January and February of 2007 were exceptionally cold months and the gas bill was enormous when it arrived in March. They put it on the mantlepiece and tried to forget about it. The same with the electricity bill.

Gary and Sue's action plan
The rest of the story is sadly inevitable. The arrears on the mortgage built up. The utility companies threatened to cut off services and the credit card company refused to accept further charges to the card until the backlog of minimum payments had been made.

They had to have gas and electricity in a house with a young child so they agreed to prepaid meters charged at a higher rate per unit until the arrears were paid off. The bank saw that they were in trouble and ended the overdraft facility. It also immediately deducted the full amount of the overdraft, plus outstanding interest, from Gary's April salary cheque. This left precisely nothing in the account for the rest of the month. The building society warned them that unless they got their interest payments up to date they would start repossession proceedings.

Gary and Sue went to see the building society, which told them they would not press for arrears for six months, provided the current payments were kept up to date. The building society thought this was a reasonable offer, but with no money to pay the April interest payment, Gary and Sue almost immediately defaulted on the agreement. Repossession proceedings started.

Sue had got into arrears with payments to the child-minder too. The lady was sympathetic for a month or so, but when she saw things were going from bad to worse, she told Sue she couldn't take the baby any longer. Sue had to give up her part-time work.

We don't need to go into the gruesome details of the final months of 2007. They tried putting the house on the market to downsize to a smaller and cheaper house. But the housing market was now very different from 2003. Prices had started to fall and there were no buyers. The estate agent estimated that to be certain of a sale they would have to drop the price to £210,000: £10,000 more than they paid for it, but a lot less than they owed the building society. When the interest arrears were added to the £215,000 borrowed, they were trapped in negative equity.

2008

By mid 2008 Gary and Sue's house had been repossessed and they were living in a small, rented flat in a far from salubrious area. They had trouble getting credit for anything. They wondered where they had gone wrong.

Where Gary and Sue went wrong

Of course, with the benefit of hindsight, we can see clearly where they went wrong.

♦ They went for the biggest mortgage they could afford on an interest only basis when interest rates were at a historically low basis. They did not take account of the fact that a significant amount of Gary's salary was bonus which could be cut without notice. When interest rates went up their payments went up by a far greater percentage than would have been the case if they had had a repayment mortgage.

♦ They did not consider whether they could pay their mortgage and credit card bills if their circumstances changed – e.g. Sue becoming pregnant.

♦ They allowed a large amount of long-term debt to build up on their credit cards at a high rate of interest.

♦ Despite rising interest rates, they increased their already high mortgage to pay for something that was going to fall in value – a new car.

♦ They did not have an emergency savings fund to cope with emergencies.

JANET AND JOHN: HOW THEY TRIUMPHED OVER ADVERSITY

February 2007

Janet and John sat down one evening in February 2007 when the weather outside was as black as the prospect facing them inside. June was safely tucked up in her cot and fast asleep, and they could have two or three hours undisturbed to look at their problems and find some solutions.

Janet and John's action plan

It was obvious to them which was the first decision to be taken. John was now at home during the day. He was sending out CVs to everyone he could think of in his line of work, but he had only had two interviews in the past two months – neither of which was successful. He could therefore look after June all week and they would save £280 per month in child minding costs. What, though, if he got a few interviews? Janet thought her mother and father (who was now retired) could, between them, look after June (indeed would enjoy doing so) for the odd day every now and again.

They had a cup of coffee to celebrate the first positive decision and then settled down to work again.

Reducing mortgage costs

John got onto the internet to see if he could find a significantly cheaper mortgage provider to cut their monthly repayments. As soon as he started, he realised what until then he had not thought of. Everyone offered interest-only mortgages. Without capital repayments, even at the same rate of interest that they were paying, the monthly payments were almost £250 per month lower, £762 per month instead of £982 per month. (The outstanding balance was down from £152,500 to £150,000.) Even if his existing mortgage provider wouldn't offer them a switch to interest only there were plenty out there who would.

Looking at personal loan repayments

Janet and John looked at their personal loan agreement. There didn't seem much prospect of saving anything here. The payments of interest and capital were firmly fixed. Even early repayment carried heavy penalties. So even if they were able to fix up a replacement interest-only mortgage for a larger amount than their existing one, the lower interest rate compared with the personal loan would be cancelled out by the penalties. The personal loan was from their own bank, though, and they had been good customers for several years. John thought it might be worth ringing them in the morning to see if they would agree to suspend the capital repayments for a few months and accept an interest-only repayment period.

Cutting costs

Then they started looking at their transport arrangements. Obviously Janet needed her car to get to and from work. But John's car had been a company car, and his employer had let him have it at a very advantageous price with part of his salary in lieu of notice. It was three years old and was still worth a few thousand. The question was, could they do without it? Of course they could. If he got an interview which he couldn't get to on public transport, he could drive Janet to work in her car, drop off June at her grandparents and then go off to the interview in Janet's car.

That would save the running cost of a car – petrol, insurance and car tax – about £80 per month even for the low mileage he did in it. It would also give them £3,000 or so to keep them going until he found a job, or for any other nasty surprises which fate might have in store for them.

The next morning, John rang their building society. They were surprisingly helpful. Yes, they could switch to an interest-only mortgage at the same rate of interest. The monthly payments would go down from £982 per month to £762 per month. There were no additional survey or legal fees – something he would probably have had to pay in one form or another if he had gone to another lender. Of course, if he had shopped around he might have found a lender with a lower rate of interest, which might have more than compensated for the up front charges. But with all their current worries, they preferred to stay with the lender they knew. Customer loyalty comes at a price – often to the customer!

Their bank was a lot less helpful. No, they couldn't do anything about reducing the payments on the personal loan to interest only. If Janet and John had temporary cash flow problems, they would be willing to offer an authorised overdraft facility – at 16% plus set up fees. 'No thanks!' said John.

Already they had reduced their essential costs by over £600 per month by John looking after the baby, switching to an interest-only mortgage and giving up one car.

Making further savings
But they knew there were further savings to be made. They decided to create a household budget and look at what was essential, what was desirable and what they could cut down on. (Full details of how to create a personal budget can be found on page 80.) Here is what they found.

They had already dealt with the mortgage payments and had decided there was nothing they could do at present on the personal loan repayments. Nor could they do anything about council tax. (Although had Janet's income been lower they would have qualified for a council tax rebate.)

Water was worth looking at though. If they got a water meter installed they might easily save something – they did not use water on the garden and they usually showered rather than bathing. The water company told them they would probably save at least 20% on their water bill, and they were in a period where installation was for a nominal amount rather than the usual quite high charge.

There were probably economies they could make on gas and electricity by switching suppliers. John was home with the baby all day, so the gas central heating bill was likely to go up rather than down even if they turned off radiators in rooms they weren't using. Putting in thicker roof insulation could help keep down the increase too and would cost very little to install with John doing it himself.

They could save on electricity by making sure they turned off lights in the rooms they weren't using and not leaving the TV and video on standby. They knew they had been very careless about this in the past. And saving on gas and electricity was good for the environment. Save the planet and save money too!

They looked at their life insurance policy – could they stop paying or reduce that? No. June's future was too important for that.

Food was the other essential. At least, most of it was. But there were a lot of things in the weekly supermarket shop which were not strictly essential and which could be reduced until times got better. Own brand goods were also usually cheaper than advertised brands. They also went to a cheaper supermarket and avoided prepared meals. By looking at what they usually got they found they could save £20 per month.

Holidays and clothes were another obvious target. They would have made savings on cinema and other leisure activities, but since June had been born they hadn't had either the time or the energy for much of that.

There were savings to be made on their phone bills. They both had mobiles – John's inherited from his company. He had taken over the rental agreement. That could go – one in the family when they were out was enough. They also shopped around with phone providers, and found that due to the pattern of their calls, they could get a cheaper deal from another provider without cutting back on calls.

Taking all their non-essential expenditure into account, including plans to take self-catering holidays in the UK out of season, rather than overseas in a hotel as they had done in the past, Janet and John found they could make savings of a further £200 per month.

Still though, there was a gap between what was going in and what was going out. True, the £3,000 they got from selling the car would help tide them over several months, and John might get a job in that time. There again, he might not.

Increasing income
They had done all they could on the expenditure side of the equation, but they hadn't looked at the income side. Perhaps they could increase that. Janet could do overtime – the NHS was always desperate for qualified staff to do extra shifts. But she was already exhausted with the hours she did now and she didn't want to spend any more time away from the baby.

But John had skills which could be used in a number of ways outside a conventional full-time job. One or two acquaintances had already asked him to help them with problems they had with their home computers. He had fixed them quite easily, and they had bought him a drink or two in appreciation. He decided he might be able to do this on a more regular basis in the evenings when Janet was at home to look after the baby. He put a card in the local newsagent's window and quickly got two or three responses. With just a couple of evenings' work a week, John found he could earn £160 per month – and because this amount was within his personal tax free allowance, he could declare it and still get it tax free.

They also noticed newspaper adverts about the government's Children's Tax Credit and the Working Tax Credit. Janet's income was just too high to qualify for the Working Tax Credit. But they were entitled to tax credits for June and this raised Janet's income by £40 a month. They also asked for it to be backdated the maximum three months.

July 2007

So when in July 2007 they decided to have another hard look at their finances, Janet and John found that their prospects were a lot brighter than they had been six months earlier, despite the fact that their basic circumstances had not fundamentally changed since John had lost his job.

Overview of Janet and John's situation

Two factors had led to their success in bringing their situation back under control.

First, they had been cautious about debt and spending from the outset. They had not bought the most expensive house or the biggest mortgage that they could afford at that time. They had left themselves some headroom in case things went wrong. And when things did go wrong, they did not panic. They thought through their situation carefully, looked for the opportunities to cut expenditure, talked to their lenders. Other factors helped. They avoided credit and store card debt, and Janet had secure and flexible employment.

They learnt some valuable lessons too. Always look at small print on insurance and other contracts, and don't expect banks and insurance companies to look after your interests. They will only be looking after their own interests once a customer is in trouble.

" It's definitely small print. "

As it turned out, later that summer John found another full-time job at nearly the same salary as he had been on before, and Janet and John lived happily ever after.

GWEN THE GRADUATE
Dicing with debt and how she escaped a fate worse than death.

September 2004
It is September 2004. Gwen is a young graduate from Bristol University who, after a gap year, has started a job as a management trainee with a telecoms company in Manchester. Her starting salary is £18,000. She has rented a house with two friends on a six months assured shorthold tenancy.

Gwen has £12,000 of student loans to repay, an out-standing credit card balance of £1,600 and she owes her parents £2,000 which she borrowed to finance her gap year in the Far East.

March 2005

Six months after they move in, one of her friends moves out after a row with the other two. Gwen and her flatmate Sarah do not expect problems in finding another tenant. However, there is by now a surplus of rented accommodation for 'professionals' in that part of Manchester and there is no taker for the vacancy.

The two girls get into difficulty with paying half the rent each, rather than one third. Soon they are in arrears with the rent and Gwen is building up credit card debt.

In order to get a third tenant, they have to agree to lower the share of the rent for the new tenant to a quarter rather than a third of the total rent. Gwen and her friend have problems in finding money for the gas and electricity bills as well as the rent. Gwen is up against the limit on her credit card and applies for another card from a different provider to get more credit.

September 2005

Six months later Gwen and her friend are in real trouble. They are under notice to quit for arrears of rent. The gas and electricity companies have installed pre-payment meters with the unit charge at double the normal rate to collect the arrears. Sarah is up to the credit limits on both her credit cards. She is finding it hard to meet even the minimum monthly payment. Their council tax is in arrears.

Gwen is reluctant to tell her parents of her difficulties and, even if she did, they could probably only help her with advice as they are by no means wealthy and she already owes them £2,000.

She is jointly liable with the other tenants who signed the original lease and electricity supply agreements to pay the outstanding amounts, including council tax. The third tenant has disappeared and so the two of them are, in practice, 'jointly and severally' liable for the whole amount. They go to the Citizens' Advice Bureau for help. They get immediate advice on how to respond to the Notice to Quit, but there is a one-month waiting list for the specialist advice they need on their debt problems. When they get to see the Debt Advisor, she sets out what they need to do to get on top of their problems.

Gwen's action plan
Acting on CAB advice:

◆ Gwen and Sarah prepare personal budgets showing income and outgoings for all essentials, demonstrating from this what they can afford to pay to creditors.

◆ They are advised to concentrate on paying their rent to ensure they keep a roof over their heads.

◆ They negotiate with the gas and electricity companies, using their personal budgets to show they can only afford to pay off their arrears at a low rate for six months.

◆ Gwen herself negotiates with her bank and the other credit card company – again using her personal budget to prove that what she is offering to pay is the most she can afford. The bank and the other credit card company know that a County Court would use the same basis to assess what she could pay and agree to the figure she has demonstrated is the most she can pay. They warn her that if she defaults on that minimum payment, she will get a County Court summons without further notice.

◆ She agrees with her fellow tenant who originally signed the lease that they will negotiate with their landlord to pay the current rent and make a contribution towards arrears. On this basis, the landlord suspends the application to the court for eviction, provided they maintain the agreed level of payments – which they do. Gwen realises how important it is to avoid a County Court Judgement against her if she is to avoid problems with getting credit (or a mortgage) in the future. Neither does she want her employer to know of her problems – which the employer would if she got an 'attachment of earnings' order against her from the Court.

◆ She explains her situation to the student loan provider, but because her income is above the level at which student loans have to start to be repaid, they are not prepared to reduce the level of payments.

The immediate crisis has been avoided by staying calm and rational. Time has been gained to get expenditure back under control. Gwen and her housemate will have a very difficult year or two with only enough money, after paying all the agreed amounts to her creditors, to eat and keep the house reasonably warm. There is virtually no money left for discretionary spending and they accept that any social life must be planned to involve no significant spending.

When Gwen gets to the end of her management training period, she gets a big pay rise with her first full management post and she begins to see light at the end of the tunnel.

Overview of Gwen's situation
The lessons she learnt are:

◆ Entering an agreement (lease, loan contract, etc) jointly with another person or people makes each individual liable for the whole amount if the others don't pay for their share.

- They could have given up the flat after the first six months of the lease had expired, and the remaining two friends could have looked for a smaller, cheaper flat.

- The burden of debt acquired as a student is considerable – particularly if some of it is on a credit card. Unless this is under control, living independently on a low salary is going to be very difficult – particularly if something unexpected happens.

LESSON FROM OUR CASE STUDIES

So we see from Janet and John, Gary and Sue and Gwen how easy it is to get into problems. We also see that it is possible, with a lot of time, worry and care, to get out of them.

The rest of the book goes into a lot more detail about how to avoid problems in the first place. It also tells how, if you can't avoid problems, you can sort them out.

In particular it looks at:

- Borrowing for house purchase – how to get the best deal.

- Other types of credit and how to avoid the pitfalls and traps set by lenders to make sure they make more money out of you.

- What to do if you do get into a financial mess.

$$\boxed{2}$$

Living with Credit – Not on It

BORROWING WITHOUT THE BAILIFFS

We've seen with Janet and John and the others how events in our lives can affect our personal finances in a dramatic way. But we've also seen how, by carefully thinking through the problems, we can solve them.

It is important to understand what we are doing when we borrow, and to plan the best ways to borrow for particular purposes whether it be a house purchase, buying a car, or a new kitchen.

CREDIT – A PINT DOWN THE PUB OR A DANGEROUS DRUG?

It can be either. Lenders – banks, building societies or credit card companies – might be no worse than pub landlords anxious to make an honest bob. But they often continue to serve drinks to customers who have had one too many. Gary and Sue's lenders did this.

Too many are more like your friendly neighbourhood drug dealer. They see someone who needs a bit of a lift and offer him 'introductory free credit' – '0% on your credit card'. You take it and feel fine. Then you need a bit more. This time there is a lot of interest to pay – and you are on the hook. As your total debt goes up, and the interest charges with it, you need more and more credit to stay afloat. You might go to another lender. Someone might offer to 'consolidate' your debts – at a higher rate of interest or with big 'administrative charges'.

Sooner or later you can't or won't pay any more. That's when the lender/dealer starts turning nasty. First come the threatening letters, then the phone calls and the Court summonses. Finally they send the boys – or bailiffs – round to sort you out.

A bit of an exaggeration, perhaps. But it is very easy to become dependent on credit unless you are absolutely clear about:

- why you are borrowing
- the type of loan you want
- how much it will cost you
- the detailed terms and conditions of the loan
- who you are borrowing from.

Let's look at each of these in turn.

WHY ARE YOU BORROWING?

As a general rule you should *not* borrow to pay for your day to day living costs. You should only borrow for a major item which will give you benefits for a number of years – a house, a car, a big domestic appliance.

TYPES OF LOAN

There are many different ways to borrow. The main ones are:

- mortgages
- second mortgages
- personal 'unsecured' loans from a bank
- overdrafts – 'authorised' and 'unauthorised'
- credit cards
- hire purchase
- store cards
- store credit/extended credit/free credit
- catalogue credit
- doorstep credit
- credit unions.

We will look at each of these different types of credit later in Chapter 4.

HOW MUCH WILL IT COST TO BORROW WHAT YOU NEED?

There are huge differences in the costs of different types of loan. A mortgage for house purchase might be as little as 4% per annum while doorstep credit can be up to 200%

per annum. The differences between lenders for the same type of credit can be much bigger than you might think. *It always pays to shop around.*

Just as important as the rate of interest are the **terms and conditions**. The small print can contain conditions which will add a lot to the overall cost of the loan – administrative charges, penalties, minimum loan periods, charges for early repayment – even compulsory insurance against redundancy. *Always read the small print before you sign up.*

First, let's look a bit more closely at interest rates and in particular some of the tricks banks get up to. They are trying to make the deals they are offering look a lot more attractive than they really are.

When you are looking for ways of borrowing money (or saving it for that matter) you come across a whole range of technical terms. They are used by companies to confuse you rather than inform you. You will probably want to throw your hands in the air and say 'that's too complicated – I'll take the deal with the lowest rate in the advert.' Don't! That's exactly what they want you to do.

The figure to look for is the **APR (annual percentage rate)**. This figure is an attempt to provide a standardised method of calculating interest charges so that people can compare like with like. Unfortunately it has not turned out quite as simple as that. It recently took a Cambridge mathematician several hours to work out exactly how the APR quoted by a major UK bank had been calculated.

But APR is probably the nearest you will get to finding a way of comparing lenders' rates, so this is the one to look for. In Appendix A5 you will find a table showing the monthly payments you should expect for various sizes of loan over different periods at different annual percentage rates (APRs). The table also shows the *total* amount of interest you would pay over the whole period. This will show you how much extra you pay on a long-term loan with a difference of only 1 or 2 % in the APR.

It's not the only rate that you will see quoted though. Many mortgage lenders quote a very low looking rate in large type and then put a different (and higher) APR figure underneath it in smaller print. Ignore anything other than APR.

Base rate is also mentioned. You will often read that a variable rate will be 1 or 2 % **above base rate**. Base rate is linked to **minimum lending rate (MLR)**. MLR is the minimum rate at which the Bank of England is prepared to lend to other banks. That may not sound as though it matters much to you. It is, though, the basis on which all other rates of interest are charged by banks and building societies. You may be surprised by how much base rate has gone up and down over the years. This is important because in recent years interest rates have been fairly stable and in historical terms, very low. *Since 1990, minimum lending rate has ranged between 3.75% and 15%.* You should think hard, therefore, about what would happen to your finances if rates went up to even 6% or 7%.

WHO ARE YOU BORROWING FROM?

Don't borrow from loan sharks. Easy to say, but how do you recognise them? They don't come with white teeth and fins when you are looking for a loan. Some very gentle looking old trout can turn out to be a great white. Building societies are mostly OK. But banks are a different matter altogether. Some of the biggest and most well known banks are the sharpest operators. Forget the image of the friendly 'high street' banks, which they spend millions on cultivating in TV adverts. Remember, you, the borrower, are paying for that advertising. The banks are there to make as much money out of you for their shareholders as they possibly can. Sure, there is a Code of Banking Practice. But that doesn't stop some banks from making loans which are very close to daylight robbery. So check out what they are offering you very carefully. Don't be taken in by the charming, smiling woman at the desk in the plushly carpeted reception area (you're paying for the carpet too). Check the small print of any leaflet she gives you and ask the right questions. (See Questions to Ask on page 72.)

$$\left(\begin{array}{c}3\end{array}\right)$$

Buying the Dream Home: How to Get the Right Deal

BUT FIRST – SHOULD YOU RENT OR BUY?

Before you decide on the best way to finance buying a house, let's first consider whether that is the right thing to do, or whether renting might be better.

There are, of course, non-financial factors which will affect the decision to rent or buy.

- How mobile do you need to be?
- Do you want the responsibility of ownership and all the hassle that goes with it?

But let's assume the non-financial factors point to deciding on the basis of purely financial reasons.

If you were to rent an unfurnished, three-bedroomed, semi-detached house in a pleasant residential area of a city like Sheffield, you would probably have to pay rent of around £600 per month. That is a total of £180,000 over 25 years. And that assumes that the rent doesn't go up during that period – which of course it almost certainly will.

If you bought the identical house for £165,000, with a deposit of £15,000 and a mortgage of £150,000 at 5.2%

p.a., you would pay £894 a month in interest and capital repayments. Over the 25 years you would repay a total of £268,335, of which £118,335 would be interest. The interest is £61,665 less than the rent paid and you own the house debt free at the end of 25 years. Of course, interest rates could go up just as easily as rent – but this example assumes neither changes.

Of course, it's not as simple as this. There are other costs as well as benefits in buying compared with renting:

Benefits

◆ Interest payments may be less.

◆ You get the benefit of any increase in the money value of the property.

Costs

◆ There are 'up front' costs in buying a house (stamp duty, legal fees, etc).

◆ You have to pay building insurance as well as contents insurance.

◆ You are responsible for property repairs.

◆ You lose out if the property falls in value.

◆ If the money value falls below the amount of the loan outstanding, you are in **negative equity** and the lender may demand repayment of some of the loan capital.

◆ If your income falls, through illness or unemployment, Housing Benefit is less generous in helping with mortgage interest than with rent.

SO YOU'VE DECIDED TO BUY

A mortgage is the cheapest type of credit you are ever going to be offered. The interest is usually only 1 or 2% above base rate – and in some 'introductory offers' may actually be below it for the first two or three years.

The reason the interest rate is lower than for other forms of credit is that the loan is **secured** on the property on which the loan is given. This means that if you get behind with the payments, the bank or building society that lent you the money can throw you out of the house and sell it to raise the money you owe them. They may give you back anything left over from selling the house after they have taken the money owing, plus interest, plus 'charges'. But they usually ensure that their 'charges and expenses' are so high that they can keep the lot.

So the lender has very little risk in lending you money secured on a house. People can do a 'moonlighter' to avoid their other debts, but they can't take the house with them!

Because you are borrowing on a mortgage over a long period – often 25 years or more – the interest you pay will add up to a great deal of money. As we've seen, if you borrow £150,000 at an APR of 5.2% for 25 years you will repay a total of £268,335 over the 25 years. £118,335 of that will be interest payments.

In exchange for the interest payments, you have the benefit of the use of the house before you have paid for it. So you can look at that £118,335 as a form of rent paid for the right to occupy the house, while the capital repayments of £150,000 are what you pay to actually buy it.

As we have seen, with interest rates as low as they are in the early years of the twenty-first century, the amount of interest you pay will often be quite a bit less than the rent you would pay as an unfurnished tenant in a similar property.

FINDING THE BEST MORTGAGE DEAL

Having decided to buy, you need to work out which of the many hundreds of mortgage deals on offer you are going to take.

The deals on offer change almost daily so there is no point in me telling you which is the 'best buy' here. What I can do is tell you the types of deal which are around and suggest the things you should be looking out for to find the best buy yourself.

First, it makes sense to get advice from a mortgage broker/financial adviser. The estate agent you are buying the house through will probably suggest one, but you are under no obligation to go to that one. There are plenty around and word of mouth recommendation from a friend or colleague is probably the best bet. Remember, though, that you don't have to take the advice you get.

The adviser is going to get a fairly fat commission on any deal you take through him or her. It could (but it shouldn't) affect the advice you get.

Whatever the advisor does recommend, it is wise to check it out yourself before you accept it. There are now a lot of websites offering a 'find the best buy service'. You enter all the details about yourself and the house you want to buy, together with the type of mortgage (see below) you want, and the website will come up with the best buy for the particular circumstances.

" Why don't you recommend Loamshire Building Society ? It's ¼% cheaper. "

If this is different from the one the adviser is recommending – particularly if it looks a better deal – then go back to the adviser and ask why they are not recommending it. There may be a good reason linked to your particular circumstances. But if they don't come up with a convincing explanation, look for another adviser.

Some of the websites offering best buy information are:

◆ www.guardian.co.uk/money
◆ www.motleyfool.co.uk
◆ www.investorschronicle.co.uk

The decision on your house purchase and mortgage will probably turn out to be the single most important financial decision of your life. Let's look hard at the way you need to approach that decision.

HOW BIG A HOUSE AND HOW BIG A MORTGAGE?

The advice on this question which was given to us by a very wise old uncle in the 1960s was 'Buy the most expensive house that is right for you and on which you can afford to pay the mortgage'. That proved excellent advice at the time and probably continued to be good advice right up until the 1990s. The reasons for that were:

◆ House prices rose fairly steadily throughout the period (with one blip in the early 1990s).

◆ There was tax relief on mortgage interest payments for a lot of that period.

◆ General prices (inflation) were rising at a fast rate throughout the period. Often interest rates were actually below the rate of price rises (they rose as much as 15–25% in one or two years in the 1970s and early 1980s, see section on real or nominal interest rates, page 70, if you want to get your head round that one). So if you were a borrower, part of your loan was really being paid for by savers whose savings were shrinking in value even though they appeared to be getting high rates of interest on them (12–15% p.a.). The effect of all this was dramatic. You bought a three-bedroomed house in the South East of England for £12,000 in 1975 with a mortgage over 25 years of £10,000. If you were on average wages, the repayments represented about 30% of your after-tax monthly income. By 1990, your repayments were only 5% of your monthly after-tax income and your house was worth £200,000 and you only owed £3,000 to the building society! Your net worth had increased by £197,000!

But would I give the same advice to my son or daughter, nephew or niece today? As always, the answer is 'It depends', but I would certainly be a lot more cautious in what I said because the world has changed an awful lot in the last ten years. It is very unlikely that my children's generation of house buyers are going to be as lucky as us.

The main changes are:

- There is no tax relief on mortgage interest payments.

- House prices have gone up faster than *ever* before in recent years. They cannot go on rising at that rate and could fall back as they did in the early 1990s.

- Interest rates are currently low by the standards of the last 50 years. This has meant that repayments on the average mortgage as a proportion of borrowers' incomes are very low compared with earlier years.

Whereas in the 1970s it was unusual to get a loan of more than 2½ times your salary, in 2004 loans of three or four times salary were not difficult to get. That is fine and affordable if interest rates stay low. But if they go up and a lot of people are forced to sell their houses and switch to a smaller or cheaper house, there is only one way house prices can go. That is down.

◆ Since the late 1990s overall price increases (inflation) have been at their lowest levels for some 50 years. If this continues, the size of outstanding mortgages will only be reduced by capital repayments and not by inflation as they were over the years 1965 to 1995.

Obviously, the decision you take will depend on the type of house you need, but you have a choice to make with that as well.

◆ Do you go for the most expensive house and the biggest mortgage you can afford?

◆ Or do you make sure you keep back some savings and have cash to spare from your salary each month for other things?

You will have saved for the deposit on the house and now you will have to decide if you want to put all your savings into the purchase or hold some back for decorating, furnishing and emergencies. You may need some for repairs or alterations before you move in. The lender may not put up the money for these. If the house is old or in poor repair, the lender may limit the mortgage to 75 or 80% of the purchase price. You will have to put up the other 20 or 25%.

The decision you take will probably depend on whether you are cautious or bold in your financial behaviour.

Here are some of the points you will want to keep in mind in reaching your decision:

◆ The smaller the loan is as a percentage of the house value, the better the deal you are likely to get from the lender in terms of interest rates, fees and the length of the discounted interest rate period.

◆ What is the condition of the house? Even if it seems OK it is always best to keep a sizeable amount of cash standing by in case something nasty creeps out of the woodwork (literally), or other things like the central heating boiler go wrong or the roof starts leaking.

◆ If your mortgage interest rate goes up, you have got bigger problems if you have stretched yourself to the maximum loan available.

◆ On the other hand, the higher the percentage you borrow, the bigger the return on the cash you have put into the house if the value of the house rises. *But remember, if house prices fall, the amount you have to pay back stays the same even if the house is worth less.*

There are also events and circumstances not directly connected to the house you choose that you ought to think about when deciding how big a loan to take out:

◆ Do you expect (rather than just hope) to be on a much higher salary in say ten years' time (ignoring inflation)?

- How safe is your job? If you are relying on overtime or bonuses to pay the mortgage, how certain are you of getting extra money over and above basic pay for quite a few years ahead?

- If you are self-employed you should be able to find a mortgage lender who requires only one year's business accounts as evidence of income. In the past, lenders required a minimum of three years' accounts, signed off by an accountant. You may find a lender offering to base the mortgage on self-certified income. But look hard at the interest rate and the small print – this type of mortgage may cost you more.

- When might you *need* to replace your car or some other major item?

- Are you considering private education for the children? How much will that cost and when will it start?

- If you are married or in a long-term relationship, do you need both incomes to keep up with the mortgage payments? If so, what if extra domestic responsibilities come along – not just babies, but dependent elderly relatives?

- Are you and your partner in good health? It could affect both your jobs if one of you is not.

- How secure is the partnership? It's sad to have to mention this, but this is one of the most common causes of default on mortgage payments and losing the family home. You may say, 'don't be daft, we wouldn't be buying a house together if we thought the marriage was on the rocks'. But some people buy a home because they think it will help patch up a rocky marriage. And remember, after bereavement and divorce, buying and selling a house is the most stressful life event – so it could even cause the marriage to break up!

After you have thought about all of these points, you should choose your house on the basis of where and how you want to live, provided you can afford it. The decision should not be made part of a strategy of growth investment. *If you choose a house that you like and you can afford to pay the mortgage, it doesn't actually matter very much if house prices fall. You will still have somewhere to live.*

WHAT TYPES OF MORTGAGE ARE THERE?

There are lots of different names used for mortgages, but essentially there are four basic types.

Standard variable rate mortgages (SVR)

This is the simplest, but not usually the best value, type of mortgage offered by lenders. It is linked to **base rate** (go back to page 38 if you've forgotten what that is), and goes up and down with base rate. You are not likely to be tied to it for any fixed period or pay penalties if you repay it early.

Discounted variable rate

This is the rate used to draw in new borrowers, particularly first time buyers. It offers a starting rate at a considerably lower rate than the SVR for a fixed period. This discounted rate is often very attractive, sometimes even below base rate. Despite the discount, the rate will still go up and down as base rate goes up and down. There are usually penalties discouraging early repayment during this initial period. At the end of the discounted rate period, the interest rate charged rises to the lender's SVR. At that point, there is usually nothing to stop the borrower switching to another lender for a new 'discounted rate'. The lender relies on the borrowers' loyalty or more usually laziness not to switch lender at this point. It is surprising how many people don't get round to switching.

Fixed rate

Most lenders offer a mortgage at a rate of interest fixed for up to five years. There are a small number of lenders who offer rates fixed for the whole period of the loan. The initial rate is usually different to the SVR – lower if at the time you are buying interest rates are expected to fall, higher if they are expected to rise.

At a time when interest rates are expected to rise, it may well be worth paying the extra if the fixed rate period is a long one – say five years. The extra peace of mind of knowing exactly what you are going to have to pay regardless of what happens to interest rates may well be worth paying a little extra for. Whether you choose this type depends on how important it is to you to have certainty for a period.

During the fixed rate period there are usually stiff penalties for paying off the mortgage early. So if interest rates suddenly start to fall, you could be paying a higher rate than necessary. At the end of the fixed rate period, the interest rate reverts to whatever the lender's SVR is at that time. But at this point, you are usually free to shop around for a better deal.

Capped rates

This sometimes seems the best of both worlds. With a capped rate, you usually start somewhere near the lender's SVR. It is often described as being linked to base rate (e.g. base rate + 1%). If base rate goes down, the capped rate goes down with it. But if it rises it will only rise as far as the 'cap'. The cap will usually be above the existing SVR. For example, if base rate is 4.5%, the lender's SVR is 6% and capped rate is base rate +1½ % (6¼%), the cap might be set at 7.5%. Even if base rate rose to 8% during the period of the 'cap' (often up to five years) and SVR became 9%, you would still only pay 7.5%.

This type of rate limits the risk if you think interest rates will rise. But you will have to pay more at the time you take out the mortgage than you would for the best discounted variable rate deal. You are, in effect, paying a form of insurance against big rate rises. As with the other types of 'non-standard' mortgage you usually have to pay a penalty if you repay during the capped period.

In addition to these four most common types of mortgage, there are a number of other special deals about.

+ **Flexible mortgages**. These allow you to pay off part of the mortgage early if you find yourself with spare cash. They also let you suspend payments for a period if you have to. Some banks let you link your mortgage to your bank account, so that when you are in credit on your current account, the amount on which you pay interest on your mortgage is reduced by the amount in your current account.

◆ **Low start mortgages**. If you are certain your finances will improve over the first few years of the mortgage, a low start mortgage will allow lower payments in the early years and a higher rate later on. They are designed for young professionals whose earnings are low early in their career, then rise rapidly. There are big penalties for early repayment for obvious reasons.

◆ **Cash back mortgages**. These give you more money up front to cover removal expenses, legal fees, decoration and similar costs of moving into a new home. But it's not for free – you are in effect borrowing a higher percentage of the value of the house. And you may be paying a higher interest rate than you need to as well. Be wary of them.

So it is a bit of a maze (see Figure 1). There isn't a best buy for the *type* of mortgage on offer – you must decide on the basis of your own attitude to risk and your individual circumstances. There will be a best buy within each type of mortgage and a good financial advisor will tell you what that is at the particular time you need to take out a mortgage.

Repayment mortgage or interest only?

Most mortgages are on a repayment basis. Your monthly payment is part repayment of the loan and part interest. In the early years of the mortgage, by far the greater part of the payment is interest, but as the outstanding capital gradually reduces, a greater and greater proportion of the monthly payment is repayment of the loan.

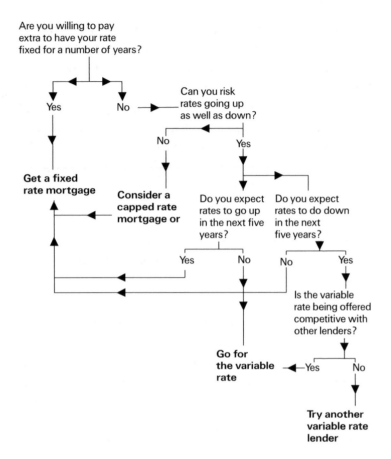

Figure 1. Find your way through the mortgage maze.

It is possible, however, to get a mortgage on an interest only basis. These used to be linked with endowment life assurance policies. However, endowment policies have fallen into disrepute as many have failed to perform well enough to pay off the mortgage loan capital at the end of the loan period.

With interest only mortgages, the monthly payment is obviously smaller than with a repayment mortgage for the same amount borrowed. But you have got to have a plan to pay off the capital at the end of the mortgage period. For example, you might plan to use the tax free lump sum you expect to receive from your pension when you retire. You might have your own investments and savings which you plan to use to pay off the loan. You might plan to sell your house at the end of the mortgage period and downsize to a smaller and cheaper one – using the difference in value to pay off the loan. You might have a business to sell when you retire and plan to use the sale proceeds to repay the mortgage.

All these plans do carry a big element of risk. Will your pension fund lump sum be big enough to pay off the loan? This will depend on the underlying performance of the investments in the pension fund or the salary you earn at the time of retirement if you have a salary defined pension. Will your savings and investments perform well enough to pay off the loan? Will house prices rise over the period of the loan to create a big enough difference if you downsize to pay off the mortgage? Will your business be saleable at the time you need to pay off the mortgage?

The important point to remember is that you must have a realistic plan for repayment. Don't take out an interest only mortgage because you can get a bigger loan for the same monthly payment. Without a repayment plan, you could end up homeless at the end of the mortgage period.

If you want to ensure that your mortgage will be repaid at the end of the mortgage period, a repayment mortgage is almost certainly the best option. But each individual's circumstances are different and the interest only option may be best for some people.

Watch the small print

Once you have decided on the type of mortgage which suits you best you need to move on to find the best buy. This is where it gets even more complicated. The best buy is not always the one with the lowest rate of interest. There will be important differences in the small print between deals offered by lenders even where the rate of interest remains the same. Here are some of them.

- **Early repayment penalties**. The length of time you will be 'locked in' to a particular lender and the size of the penalty you will have to pay to get unlocked will vary. It is particularly important to look at this when you have decided to go for a discounted, capped or fixed rate mortgage. For example, if mortgage rates go down when you have a fixed rate mortgage you will want to get out as soon as possible.

- **Free valuation/survey**. The lender will want a survey carried out on the property before they agree to a mortgage to ensure it is worth as much as you are paying for it. The survey is for their benefit, not yours. It is usually only a valuation and not a structural survey. (You should get your own house owner's survey done unless you are certain it is in reasonable condition.) Some lenders will offer to arrange the valuation/survey they need free, others will charge for it. Free valuation helps keep your 'up front' cost down.

- Some lenders offer a **free legal service** for drawing up the mortgage documents. Others charge a fee for it.

- Most lenders, but not all, charge a **set-up fee** (normally £200–£300).

◆ **Mortgage indemnity premium**. This insures the risk of you not paying back the mortgage and the house not being worth enough to cover the outstanding amount. You will get no benefit from this, but will have to pay the premiums. Look carefully for deals that don't require these. There are plenty around. If you are putting down a deposit of 10% or more you should not have to pay for a MIP.

◆ **Accident and unemployment insurance**. This is usually voluntary and sometimes offered free by the lender. It is meant to cover the mortgage repayments if you lose your job or don't get paid when you are ill. However, be careful if you choose to pay this yourself. The circumstances when this actually benefits you are fairly rare. You often have to be sick or unemployed as a result of *compulsory* redundancy (i.e. not leaving the job voluntarily) for a period of three or even six months before they start paying up. That doesn't happen to many people. And the payments they make may only go on for a period – not usually for an unlimited period of illness or unemployment.

ANY CLEARER?

I hope so. You can see that getting a mortgage is far from simple – one of the reasons that buying a house is such a stressful business. But the more you think through all the options, the more likely you are to make the right decision for you in your particular circumstances.

WHAT ARE SECOND MORTGAGES?

Don't confuse second mortgages with ordinary mortgages, or getting a bigger loan from your original mortgage lender. Second mortgages are expensive and they put your house at risk if you get into financial trouble.

If you have no **equity** left in your house and you need to borrow money (in other words the size of your outstanding mortgage is close to the actual value of the house) you won't be able to get a top-up to your existing mortgage.

You might be tempted by the sound of a second mortgage. This is a loan from a bank or other lender, usually at a rate of interest a lot higher than the original mortgage. It is secured on your house – but your original mortgage lender has first priority to get the money from the sale of your house if you get into difficulties. That is why it is called a second mortgage and why the interest rate is higher than on a first mortgage.

There are very few, if any, advantages to you – the borrower – in getting a loan based on a second mortgage unless you cannot find anyone to lend you money on any other basis. It is much better to go for a personal loan. It will probably be at a similar interest rate or even less than that offered on a second mortgage.

Second mortgages are best left to people whose credit record is poor, so that they have difficulties in getting 'unsecured' loans at reasonable rates of interest.

$$\left(\ 4\ \right)$$

Getting Credit: Dealing with Banks and Other Ruthless Predators

USING THE VALUE IN YOUR HOUSE TO BORROW MORE

So you need a new car, or a conservatory extension on your house, or a new kitchen or bathroom. What is the cheapest way to borrow for these things?

Let's imagine you have been living in your new home for a few years and during that time it has gone up in value by 30%. It's now worth £260,000 compared to the £165,000 you paid for it. Your outstanding mortgage (taking account of what you have paid off on your repayment mortgage) is now only £130,000. You now have £130,000 of equity in the property and you can borrow against that added value by increasing your existing mortgage. This is by far the cheapest way of borrowing money for large items.

In these circumstances, your bank or building society lender will be delighted to lend you more money, provided you have kept up to date on your mortgage repayments since you took out your original mortgage. You should be able to get the increase on the same terms as your existing mortgage. If your lender does not agree to that and you are clear of the early redemption penalty period, shop around for a new lender. You may find a financial adviser as helpful as with the original loan. There will be plenty of lenders around offering to start a brand new mortgage for the whole of your existing outstanding mortgage plus the new money you want to borrow. And you can probably start a new discounted variable rate period too. Be careful, though, if you are benefiting from a fixed or capped rate mortgage where standard variable rates are already above the fixed or capped rate which you are paying. In these circumstances you will be better off agreeing to borrow the *extra* money you need from your existing lender at the higher SVR than giving up the benefit of your fixed rate or cap on what you owe already.

Before you switch from one lender to another for a better rate, check what set-up fees, legal costs and valuation fees you may have to pay. Some lenders will negotiate on these in order to get your business. When you think you have the best deals on the up front fees and charges, make sure that they don't add up to more than any extra you will pay in interest over the remaining period of the loan if you stick with your existing lender. A good financial adviser will help you with the calculation.

PERSONAL LOANS

Perhaps you haven't been in the house long, or house prices have not risen since you bought your house. If there is no 'new equity' in the house since you originally took out the mortgage, you are going to have to look elsewhere.

The next best deal you are likely to get is a personal loan.

Personal loans are made to people with good credit records. Because they are not secured on the borrower's house, the lender will charge a higher rate of interest than they would charge on a mortgage loan. The lenders are relying on their judgement of your credit worthiness to get their money back. They will therefore carry out detailed checks with credit agencies, on your credit card record and on your current bank account. If there are problems you may not get a loan.

The high street banks are big lenders of this type and if you go to your own bank for a loan to buy a car or for a new kitchen or bathroom, this is the type of loan you are most likely to be offered. The interest rate (APR) may be at double and in some cases as much as four times what you would expect to pay for a mortgage. (So if you can raise the money through increasing your mortgage, you'll be a lot better off doing that rather than taking a personal loan.)

The loan will usually be offered for a minimum of two years and there will not be an option to repay earlier (except possibly with a big penalty). Banks prefer to lend to you for as long as possible – five or even ten years. The repayments are often front end loaded so that you will pay a higher rate of interest for the first two years than for the last three years of a five-year loan. The lender is encouraging you to keep the loan over the longer period. You will probably be offered a lower rate of interest if you agree to a longer loan period – but this will prove more expensive in the long run than a short term loan.

The temptation is to accept whatever your own bank offers you. If they don't like the way you've run your account with them over the years (the occasional unauthorised overdraft perhaps), they may charge you more than their minimum rate. It is vital to shop around. There are very big differences in what different lenders will offer to the same borrower. There are also big differences in what one lender will offer to borrowers with varying credit records. If you borrow £8,000 over five years at an APR of 7.8%, you will pay £1,250 less in interest than if your lender charges you 13.8%. A few phone calls may find a lender who is prepared to charge you less because they think they can sell you other services. And they may not find out about that unauthorised overdraft you once had and which your own bank knows all about.

Don't forget your other financial commitments though. Could you still pay your mortgage, your credit card *and* this new loan if you had a cut in overtime or bonus during the next three or five years? Repayment protection insurance is usually offered, but the benefits are very limited (similar to mortgage protection policies, see above). It's also very expensive for what is offered. On a £10,000 loan, the repayment protection policy is likely to cost £300 per year.

CREDIT CARDS – YOUR FLEXIBLE FRIENDS

Credit cards are a blessing and a curse. They are a frighteningly convenient way to pay for almost everything you buy. That is not a problem if you pay off the outstanding balance every month.

The trouble is that the monthly statement tells you that you only *have* to pay off a tiny amount each month. If you are well inside your credit limit the amount they ask for is just a token – sometimes less than 1% of the outstanding balance. Like the drug dealers, they are trying to get you hooked. Before you are tempted to pay only the minimum, it is important to realise what a high rate of interest you are paying for this very easy form of credit. The problem is the confusion, often deliberately created by the banks issuing the credit cards, around the interest rates they charge. The Chief Executive of Barclays recently admitted to a Select Committee of the House of Commons that he would advise his children not to run up debt on a credit card – it was much too expensive a way to borrow. Take the advice of someone who knows! A huge variety of cards are very heavily advertised through the press and through direct mail, quoting different interest rates.

◆ **Interest rate on credit balance transfers**. The interest rate quoted by different companies ranges from 0% – yes really! – to 3 or 4% above base rate. But this low rate applies only to the debt you transfer from other credit cards, and then only for a limited period – six to nine months is the usual maximum. This is the bait on the hook.

◆ **Interest rate on new purchases**. This is the rate you will pay over the long term and is much higher than the other rate – often 10 or 14% above base rate. That means you will be paying a rate of interest between three and four times what you pay for your mortgage.

♦ **Interest rate on cash withdrawals**. Some card issuers charge a higher rate on the part of the balance arising from cash withdrawals. There is also a fee for cash withdrawals – usually 2% of the amount withdrawn.

So if you are tempted to pay the minimum when your credit card statement arrives, ask yourself:

♦ Do you really need to borrow using your credit card when most other forms of credit are cheaper?

♦ If you do – remember to shop around for the card with the best rate. It will be worth changing as there are big variations in the rates charged.

♦ You will get the first few months after you switch card at a 0% or low rate on the balance you transfer. If you have the time and energy you might get away with switching a couple of times a year. Eventually you will have to pay the standard rate. Make sure you end up with the card with the lowest rate for new purchases.

Other points to remember about credit cards

♦ There is no need ever to pay an introductory or annual fee for a credit card.

♦ There are big penalty fees for not paying off the minimum monthly balance.

♦ If you are virtuous enough to pay off your balance in full every month, make sure you do it in plenty of time. Allow for postal delays. If you miss the date you could end up paying the penalty for missing the minimum payment as well as the interest on the balance. It is particularly easy to miss a payment when the statement comes in while you are away on holiday. The best plan is to go for a card which gives you the option to pay off the whole balance every month by direct debit from your bank account.

◆ If you use your credit card overseas, the rates of exchange used to calculate the sterling figure charged to your statement can vary. The card issuer may use a poor rate of exchange – or the rate may change between the day of purchase and the day the rate conversion is calculated. If you really need to know how much you are paying for something at the time you buy it, use cash or travellers' cheques.

HIRE PURCHASE

When you buy a car (particularly a secondhand car) or an expensive domestic appliance, the garage or store may try to persuade you to enter into a **hire purchase agreement**. The salesman will make more on selling you the hire purchase agreement than on selling you the car or appliance and so will be very persuasive. Unless you are unable to get an increase in your mortgage or an unsecured personal loan, you would be wise to avoid hire purchase. The interest rate will be higher than you would need to pay for a personal loan and the car or appliance will remain the property of the hire purchase company until all the payments have been made. If you default on the payments before you have paid one third of the amount owed, the hire purchase company can recover the goods, and you are still liable to make the remainder of the payments if there is a difference between the proceeds of the sale of the goods and the outstanding debt! If you have no alternative source of credit and are thinking of signing the hire purchase agreement, read the small print very carefully before you finally decide.

STORE CARDS

These operate in a similar way to credit cards, but use of the card is restricted to the chain of stores issuing the card. No cash withdrawals are available. The main difference between store cards and credit cards is the rate of interest charged. *It is a rip off.* For most of the best known store chains the rate is nearly double the APR charged on the more competitive credit cards. If you have a store card, pay off in full every month – by direct debit if possible. If you can't do this, use a credit card instead. And if you are up to your limit on your credit card, you are probably spending too much for your income anyway. So *stop spending*.

'FREE CREDIT' IN SHOPS

Yes, that's what it says on the windows and in the advertisements. But remember the most important pieces of financial advice ever given – 'If something looks too good to be true – it probably is', and 'There is no such thing as a free lunch'. Likewise, there is no such thing as 'free credit'. You will always end up paying for it. Here are some of the games that retailers play:

◆ Putting the cost of the free credit into the price of the goods.

◆ Where the 'free credit' is for a limited period, you pay a higher rate of interest than the market rate when you do start paying. There are often penalties for early repayment so you have to pay the higher rates for a fixed period even if you could afford to pay off the loan.

- Charging big penalties if you fail to start paying when the free credit period ends. Often no reminder is sent out until it's overdue. You might have forgotten or you might have run into hard times since you bought the goods two years earlier.

- Some shops might use a combination of all three of these.

How can you avoid being ripped off?
You might think that the obvious way is to pay cash up front and ask for a discount instead of 'free credit'. You might be lucky and find a shop with a salesman who will take you up on this offer.

But don't bank on it! Salesmen in shops offering these types of deal get a small basic salary. They make most of their income on selling credit agreements and insurance contracts for after sales breakdowns and maintenance. They will be disappointed if they've made a sale and then find you don't want the deal which will bring them the really juicy commission. If you do decide to go for the free credit, *read the small print very carefully,* and work out what the real cost of the payments of the 'free credit' deal are. Then go out and see if you can get cheaper credit elsewhere – perhaps from a personal loan.

'I haven't got time to do that', you might say. Think about this. If you can get credit at a rate just 2% cheaper than the deal you are being offered at the store on a £2,000 item, you'll be saving £120 on a three-year credit deal. *How long would it take you to earn that after tax and national insurance? Even if you are earning £20 an hour gross, it will take you eight hours to earn that £120. It won't take you anything like as long as that to ring around a few banks.*

CATALOGUE CREDIT

Catalogue credit, like store credit, can look attractive. There is often an interest free period for repayment of up to a year. You will be repaying by instalments during this period, but not paying interest on the outstanding balance. But like the stores offering interest free credit, you are paying for it through the prices of the goods. Let's be fair. Catalogues provide a very convenient way of spreading the cost of buying essentials like clothes and household goods and things for the children – particularly at Christmas time. You may have no alternative to mail order. Perhaps you can't get out or you live in a very rural area a long way from big stores. In which case, take advantage of the free credit – you are paying for it anyway.

But remember:

♦ If you go beyond the free credit period you will be paying around 30% APR on your outstanding credit balances.

♦ If you miss repayments during the free credit period you will lose the free credit deal, have to pay penalty payments and pay a high rate of interest.

♦ If you take orders for friends and relations you are taking the risk and cost if they don't pay up.

If you don't need the convenience of catalogue buying, then you will probably get better prices and a better overall deal by shopping around in department stores and specialist shops and paying cash up front.

OTHER TYPES OF CREDIT

Credit Unions
Not many people know about Credit Unions. They are usually small and local organisations run on co-operative lines whose purpose is to make small loans (no more than a few hundred pounds) to local people. Interest rates are low and the aim is to lend to people who have difficulty getting credit on reasonable terms elsewhere. Each Credit Union has limited capital reserves and can only loan out new money as old loans are paid back. *If you have a local*

Credit Union and they have money to lend, it's the best deal you are likely to get anywhere. Your local Citizens Advice Bureau can tell you how to contact them.

Door-to-door credit

Beware! This type of credit is aimed at people who are unable to get credit from anyone else. But unlike Credit Unions, the companies involved are not there to help such people. They are there to make money.

Some are reputable companies. Others are plain and simple loan sharks operating on the very fringe of the law. The problem is telling one from the other. In any case, reputable or not, the companies charge interest rates which are extortionate. The trouble is, because the amounts lent are small, the interest charges don't sound much to people desperate to get money to pay the rent or similar. But the actual APR can be anything between 100% and 1,000% p.a.

Agents go door to door to make the loans and collect repayments. However bad things seem, this type of loan will only make them worse. Don't get involved!

INTEREST RATES – SOMETHING TO THINK ABOUT

We have talked a lot about interest rates – especially SVR, APR and base rate. Unfortunately interest rates are even more complicated than we have described so far.

We just need to mention the little problem of **real** and **nominal** interest rates. You won't ever see them advertised, but it is important to understand the difference.

You pay interest as a penalty for having something now which you are not going to pay for until later. That seems fair enough. But you are also paying back the lender for taking the risk and (in the case of the last 60 years) the certainty, that when they get their money back it will not be worth as much (or buy as much) as when they lent you the money.

For example, if you are paying an interest rate of 5% on your mortgage (the **nominal** rate) and inflation is 2% p.a. – the **real** rate of interest is only 3% p.a. That doesn't sound a lot. But on a personal loan you might be paying 10% p.a. With inflation at 2% p.a. the **real** rate is 8% p.a. That is a very high real rate compared with some periods in recent times. In the 1970s for example, when inflation ran as high as 25% p.a., mortgage interest rates were at record highs of 15% but the **real** rate of interest on mortgages at that time was **minus** 10%. Home buyers in this period thought they were really suffering because of these historically high **nominal** rates of 15%. Actually they were getting a real bargain. Lenders were paying them to borrow their money!

So always calculate the **real** interest rate to work out what you are really paying.

This might seem a bit theoretical. But it is important when you are worried about the amount of mortgage still to be paid off. When inflation and interest rates were both high in the 1970s and 1980s, the real value of your mortgage debt was shrinking fast while the **money** value of your house was going up fast. Those of us lucky enough to buy our first houses in the 1960s found that our mortgage was being paid off courtesy of high inflation. With the low inflation of today, the opposite is the case. High mortgage debt will stay high in both **money** and **real** terms.

Checklist
So if you need to borrow, here is a checklist which will help keep the bailiffs at bay.

Questions to ask all lenders
1. What is the APR?

2. What is the length of the loan period?

3. Are there penalties for early repayments?

4. Are there any set up fees?

5. Is the interest rate fixed or variable over the period of the loan?

6. Is the loan secured on your home?

7. Are there penalties for missed or delayed interest payments?

8. Are there any other charges of any sort whatever?

Questions to ask yourself
1. What am I borrowing this for: a long-term item (house, car, washing machine) or to help with current living costs?

2. How secure is my job over the period of the loan?

3. What does my total debt add up to after I've borrowed this?

4. Can I afford the interest and capital repayments on this total debt if: a) my overtime or bonus is cut, or b) my partner's income is cut or disappears?

5. Is this the cheapest way for me to borrow for this purpose?

6. Is there another big item I am going to *have* to borrow for in the near future? How will this affect my ability to pay interest and pay back capital?

7. What is my long-term plan for getting out of debt?

5

Don't Panic if it All Goes Wrong

LIFE EVENTS

Very few people get into serious debt problems just by being irresponsible. OK, there are a tiny minority of shopaholics and compulsive gamblers. But the vast majority of problems arise through life events.

Family problems

The most common cause of financial difficulties is marriage or partnership break-ups – particularly where there are children involved. Two lots of accommodation cost a lot more than one: two cars are needed and so it goes on.

Health problems

Serious health problems, particularly mental health problems, are another major cause of financial difficulties. Some 600,000 people receive Incapacity Benefit from the State because they are unable to work through some sort of mental illness. Many mortgage protection insurance policies exclude the most common forms of mental illness – covering only the most severe conditions.

Employment problems

Job loss, or loss of regular overtime or bonus earnings is the next most common cause of debt problems. As we saw with Gary and Sue, if you build your lifestyle around a particular level of income without a safety margin and this turns out not to be secure income, problems are inevitable.

Interest rates

The general economic climate can also land people in trouble. Janet and John's and Gary and Sue's problems came about partly as a result of rising interest rates. These affected Gary and Sue more because they had borrowed right up to their limit, but they also made things difficult for Janet and John. More importantly, rising interest rates have an effect on house prices. This is partly because higher interest rates mean some people cannot afford to pay the resulting higher mortgage rates. First-time buyers cannot afford to take on high mortgage payments, and existing homeowners cannot afford to move upwards in the housing market.

House prices stop rising. Higher interest rates also slow down the economy generally, leading to job losses and loss of overtime which have the effect of cutting the amount of money people have available to pay the mortgage. Then as a small number of people are forced to sell their houses (perhaps to move to a cheaper house), at a time when there are few buyers around, prices start to fall.

" No insurance, no mortgage
worries... we should have
downsized years ago. "

Falling house prices

Falling house prices don't automatically cause home-owners problems. After all, you still have a roof over your head, and provided you are not forced to sell your house as a result of other problems (marriage break-up for example) the value of it doesn't matter. But if you had a 95% or 100% mortgage and the value of the house falls below what you owe your mortgage lender, you are in trouble. The lender will start getting worried and in some circumstances may ask for some of their money back. This forces more people to sell, and house prices start falling even faster. In the worst situations (as in the early 1990s), a downward spiral develops.

Falling house prices also limit the extent to which individuals can borrow more on their mortgage using the **equity** in their house. This reduces consumer spending and slows the economy even more.

Enough of the economics lecture! What I am trying to explain is that a number of different factors are all connected, and when one of these turns down, it brings a lot of other things down with it – and all at the same time.

Losing control

Even if the world around them is thriving (perhaps because it is), there will always be some people who get themselves into difficulty. The urge to spend is strong. Some of us can't resist it. Sometimes this is as a result of an urge to be generous. Some of us can't help indulging our children, or helping them out of trouble – and getting ourselves into trouble at the same time. Guaranteeing loans for friends or relations is an example of this.

However financial problems arise, they have to be dealt with. The sooner we start to tackle them, the less difficult it is to find a solution.

THE FIRST SIGNS OF TROUBLE

Before you can solve your problems, you have to recognise that you have them. The problems often creep up on us, particularly if we are reluctant to recognise them. What are they?

◆ Not paying off more than the minimum payment on the credit card. We may kid ourselves that we could pay more, but have chosen not to.

◆ Juggling between credit cards to avoid going above the credit limit on one or more of them.

◆ Slipping into unauthorised overdraft on our current account at the end of the month.

◆ Getting final demands from utility companies and having problems in paying them.

◆ Borrowing more from one lender (or credit card) to pay off another.

◆ Bank not paying direct debits through lack of funds.

The appearance of one or even two of these symptoms might just mean a temporary problem. But more than that means trouble. So what do you do when you have started to recognise you have a problem?

What you don't do is panic! Nor do you ignore it. Neither do you go to a debt management company. (For an explanation of what they are see Chapter 6.)

THREE STEPS TO SALVATION

There are three steps you have to take to find a way out of your difficulties.

Step 1 Find out how bad the problem is

This is in some ways the most difficult step to take. It means facing the problem head on – something you have probably been trying to avoid doing for months.

You have to draw up a simple personal budget setting out what income you have and what you are spending it on. There are three reasons for doing this.

First, it tells you how big a problem you have.

Secondly, it helps you check that you are not paying for things which you shouldn't be. Are there items on your credit card which you did not buy? Are the direct debits correct? Is anyone still collecting them when they should have stopped? These mistakes can and do happen and they can be very expensive.

Thirdly, it provides the basis for discussions with the people who are chasing you for payment. Remember that they are dealing with people with money problems all the time. They know they can't get money from people who have none. So they concentrate on people who have some and are spending it on other things (or repaying *other* debts). You have to convince them that what you are offering to pay them (and you must offer them something) is the absolute maximum you can afford. You also have to convince them that, where you have a number of creditors, they are getting a fair share of what you can afford to repay in total. Showing a personal budget to them is the best way of demonstrating this. We show how to create one later in this chapter.

Step 2 What can you cut back on?

Having got the budget in front of you, you must look at it carefully, calmly and above all, honestly.

Try dividing spending into three categories:

1. Spending which is fixed and cannot be reduced. Probably the only three in this category are mortgage interest payments, other loan repayments and council tax. But a working mother is entitled to include crèche or child minding costs in this category.

2. Spending on essential items such as food, transport, gas and electricity. Clearly you must spend on these items, but do you need to spend as much as you are doing at present?

3. Non-essentials. This is where you have to be ruthless and make most of the cuts. Above all, this is where you have to be honest with yourself. If things go badly you will have to go through these items with a lender or even a court official and justify why you need to spend on them. You must keep this in mind as you go through them and first justify every item of spending to yourself.

Step 3 Can you increase your income?

'I'm not daft,' you will say, 'I tried doing that when I first realised there were problems with paying off the credit card.' Well, perhaps! But did you consider every possibility?

- Increasing overtime working.

- Considering a second job in the evening or at weekends.

- Extending a useful hobby like woodworking or painting into a small money making venture by selling some of the best work.

- Checking whether you are getting every tax or social benefit to which you are entitled. There is now a system of tax credits for working families and elderly people which enables you to claim extra money through the tax and social security systems. These are in addition to child benefit and basic state pension and have to be claimed separately. Although they are mainly to benefit lower income families, the child tax credit can benefit families with incomes up to £50,000 per annum. The rules for these benefits are too complicated to describe in detail here, but the Citizens Advice Bureaux have excellent expert advisers on the new system and will help people decide whether they may be entitled to extra. These credits can be an important and significant source of extra income. There is also housing benefit, for those in rented accommodation, and help with council tax (of which more later). Think about whether you might be entitled to any of these.

HOW TO CREATE A PERSONAL BUDGET

The first thing you need to create this personal budget is information. You don't and can't keep all the information about your income and spending in your head. So first you should get together the essential sources of information:

- pay slips
- bank statements which will show both income and expenditure items
- credit card statements
- store card statements.

These records will show you the pattern of both income and spending.

Let's deal with income first. It may be there is only one source of income – wages or salary. In this case, the income side of the personal budget is simple. But there could be other items – pension or annuity payments, tax rebates, expenses repaid by employers for travel and other costs. Not all these things come in every month so it is important to refer to at least six months' bank statements, preferably a year's, to get the total picture.

You will need to look at the pattern of spending over the same sort of period. Water bills, for example, come in twice a year unless you make arrangements to pay monthly. Holiday spending might be only once a year.

Some checks to do
Before listing your spending, there are some important checks to carry out to ensure mistakes aren't being made, or you aren't paying for someone else's fun and games.

- It is important to keep a record of cash issued by cash machines when you withdraw money. If you haven't been doing this, start now! Check them against your bank statement on a monthly basis. This will ensure that no one has got your PIN number and is using it to make unauthorised withdrawals. Remember that this may not be an unknown thief but could be a friend or member of the family. But even if there is no problem of that type, it will make you realise how much you are drawing in cash each month. This may come as a shock!

◆ Keep and check all your credit card and store card slips against your monthly statements. 'You must be joking!' you say. Well, perhaps I don't do it either. But I do read the statements very carefully every month to make sure I recognise all the payments appearing, and in particular that none appear twice. It's surprisingly common for mistakes to be made by credit card companies – such as by pressing an input key twice by accident. If you don't notice it and complain, no one else will. If you see something you don't recognise, check it out with the credit card company. It takes time, but so does earning money! The fewer credit cards and store cards you have, the less trouble it is.

◆ Check your bank statement thoroughly every month. Look particularly at direct debits. Are they for the right amount? Have they been deducted more than once? This, as with credit cards, happens more often than it should. Utility (gas, electricity, telecom) companies are some of the worst culprits. In particular, check that when you cancel a direct debit, the bank stops paying it. If they don't, you have a legal right to have it immediately repaid without argument. If they argue, or ignore you, complain. If you find any mistakes at all, complain and ask for compensation from the bank. Don't allow them to intimidate or ignore you. Banks have been ripping off the public for decades!

Be honest with yourself

The vital thing about preparing a personal budget is to be honest with yourself and therefore with the people you are going to have to discuss your problems with. There is absolutely no point in creating a budget which misses out or hides a real item of expenditure. You have to include everything you think you are spending.

If problems get bad enough for Court proceedings to be started against you (see Chapter 7), the forms issued by the Court include a requirement to submit a personal budget set out on a standard form. Preparing an accurate budget now will help with that later when you may be even more stressed out!

What are you spending?

We have already decided to list items under three headings:

1. Fixed spending.
2. Essential items.
3. Non-essential items.

Anyone you have to discuss your budget with is going to be interested in the first two items. They might argue about what is essential and non-essential so you have to know why you have put a particular item in a particular category.

Fixed spending

1. **Mortgage interest payments or rent**. If you don't pay them you will end up without a roof over your head. Notice we have listed 'interest' and not total capital repayment. This is because it may be possible to negotiate a freeze on capital repayments with the lender. We look at that in more detail later.

2. **Council tax**. You'll soon be in Court if you don't pay council tax.

3. **Water**. Unless you have a meter, this is a fixed amount for the year.

4. **Childcare costs**. A lender will accept these as fixed spending assuming they are enabling the parent who is normally responsible for childcare to work full- or part-time, and thus earn more to repay what they owe.

Essential spending

There are items on which you must spend something, but not necessarily the amount that you are currently spending.

♦ **Food**. A big item, so a small saving each month will be a big help. There are bound to be luxury items in there somewhere and if you don't spot them and cut them out, someone else will. Many lenders have a 'rule of thumb' when looking at personal budgets where people are asking for 'time to pay'. Often they will allow no more than £35–£40 per person per week for food.

♦ **Gas and electricity**. You will be surprised how much you can save by turning off lights when you are not in a room, switching off the TV at the mains rather than leaving it on remote (safer too). Turn down the central heating and put an extra fleece on!

♦ **Transport**. You have to get to work, but is a car absolutely essential or can you do it by bus or train? You won't save much if you keep the car and then use public transport, as the standing costs of a car (tax, insurance, servicing, MOT, etc) are so high. But if you can do without a car altogether, the savings will be thousands a year. A lender you owe a lot of money to will need a lot of convincing that a car is essential unless you can show you have no other means of getting to work.

♦ **Cash withdrawals**. This is where you should be able to make big savings and you will be expected to. So much of the cash is discretionary spending. A cup of coffee, a drink, an impulse buy. If you want the cash you draw out to be considered essential, you'll have to show it was spent on essentials.

♦ **Clothes**. Of course clothes are essential, particularly clothes for the children. But a lender will not expect you to be spending much on new clothes at a time when you are in financial trouble – and certainly not for yourself! Try the Oxfam shop!

♦ **Telephones**. Something else we have come to regard as essential. But is that mobile really essential? In any case we can all cut out inessential calls, and make essential ones shorter. Be mean; let your friends phone you for a change.

◆ **Insurance**. It is possible to make big savings on home buildings and contents insurance by shopping around. If you are paying out on any life insurance premiums, you could ask the life company to make the policy paid up – i.e. pay no further premiums and, as a result, get reduced benefits. You could surrender it – although you may very well not get good value for it by doing this. It is worth talking to the life company about the options, which could include a temporary suspension of premium payments.

◆ **Other essentials**. There aren't many other things that a lender or Court would regard as essentials. Dentistry and prescription charges would probably count though.

Non-essentials
Everything else has to be regarded as non-essentials I'm afraid. That includes:

◆ holidays

◆ leisure activities – including trips out for the children and Sky TV subscriptions

◆ presents for family and friends

◆ furnishings and decoration for the house and garden.

What will a personal budget look like?
So how would you make all this look in a personal budget statement prepared for discussion with a lender or a Court official? Let's imagine a young family. The husband is working full-time and his wife part-time. Their joint salaries after tax and other deductions are £24,000 p.a.

Personal Budget

Annual income		£
Net joint basic salary after tax and other deductions		24,000
Overtime/bonus		2,000
Work expenses (mainly use of own car for business)		1,500
	Total	27,500

Spending

Annual fixed outgoings

Mortgage payments by direct debit (£600 p.m.)		7,200
Personal loan repayments – deducted from current a/c (£300 p.m.)		3,600
Council tax and water by direct debit (£166 p.m.)		2,000
	Total	12,800

Annual essential expenditure

Gas and electricity		1,200
Minimum payments on credit cards		2,200
Supermarket purchases of food and other essentials		7,500
Petrol/garage bills/other transport		1,200
Clothes		1,500
Telephone including mobiles		360
Insurance (house, contents and life)		900
Dentist/optician/prescriptions		300
	Total	15,160

Other spending

Cash withdrawals		2,400
Holidays		1,000
Pocket money and outings for children		800
TV licence and other miscellaneous items		500
Decorating and house repairs		500
	Total	5,200
	Total all spending	**£33,160**

Figure 2. Sample personal budget.

They have two children, aged 13 and 11. Their personal budget looks like the one in Figure 2.

Clearly they are in trouble with annual expenditure £5,660 greater than their income. If we look at it more closely we can see this is almost exactly the same amount that they are paying to their personal loan provider (£3,600 p.a.) and in minimum monthly payments on their credit cards (£2,200 p.a.), i.e. £5,800 in total.

So their current day-to-day expenditure is roughly in balance (assuming they are not building up more debt using their credit cards for normal expenditure). The problems they have now are because of debts they incurred in the past.

They will be coming under pressure from the credit card companies because they have stopped paying the minimum monthly payment. If the personal loan is from their own bank, the repayments will be taken out of their account as soon as the salary comes in. As a result their bank account will soon run out of cash each month. Direct debits will not get paid, cheques will bounce, cash machines will not pay out. Life will be very difficult. This is why the family must reach a deal with their bank to ease the repayments. This deal should leave them enough money to live a basic family life with a roof over their head and food to give their children. It can be as basic as that in serious debt cases.

In the next chapter we look at ways in which it is possible to sort these problems out without imposing too much hardship on the family.

6

If You Are in a Hole, Stop Digging

So you've got big problems – but you haven't panicked and you have taken the most important step of all. You've recognised the problems and faced up to them. Where do you go from here?

WHICH CREDITORS DO YOU PAY FIRST AND WHICH LAST?

The answer is straightforward. You try to pay off any debt which puts your home at risk. So the order should be:

◆ Keep up the mortgage payments or keep paying the rent.

◆ Pay any other debts which are secured on your house (second mortgages, secured loans).

◆ If you need your car to get to work and it is on hire purchase (which means it could be recovered by the HP Company), this should be treated as a priority debt.

◆ Pay Council Tax to avoid having to go to the Magistrates Court.

◆ Pay electricity and gas to avoid disconnection.

◆ Water is a lower priority because the water companies are not allowed by law to disconnect domestic consumers.

◆ Any other debts (unsecured personal loans, credit and store cards) which may end up in court and ultimately with the bailiffs.

Let's take a look at each in turn.

Keep paying the mortgage

The golden rule of managing financial problems is **keep paying the mortgage** – even if it means eating less! If you can't pay all the monthly repayment, then **keep talking to the mortgage lender.** Remember it's not in their interest to take you to Court if they can avoid it. They want your money, or as much of it as you can realistically afford. And they will probably be willing to wait for it.

But before you even get to that stage let's check whether there is anything you can do to pay the mortgage.

Help may be at hand with mortgage payments

◆ Have you got a mortgage protection policy and does your situation meet the terms of the policy for a pay out – compulsory redundancy and unemployment for a period before claiming, long term sickness, etc?

◆ Do you claim Income Support or Income Based Job Seekers' Allowance? If so, then you may be eligible to get at least some of the interest on the mortgage paid as benefit – provided the mortgage was taken out to buy, improve or repair the house and not for some other purpose. You will only get help with interest on the first £100,000 of your mortgage. For mortgages taken out after 1995, you will have to wait 39 weeks after claiming before getting any help. If you think you may be eligible for this help, contact the Department of Work and Pensions as soon as possible. There are some rules about standard interest rates and other unusual circumstances. There may be help available to you sooner if you have special responsibilities, e.g. you are a carer or have disabilities. These will be explained to you when you claim. If in doubt go to the Citizens Advice Bureau for help.

Here are some suggestions to make to the mortgage lender if they don't make them to you.

Endowment policies
If your mortgage is linked to an endowment insurance policy rather than a repayment mortgage, you could reduce the monthly payments by surrendering your endowment policy and switching to a repayment mortgage.

♦ First compare the cost of a repayment mortgage with what you are paying for the endowment mortgage (both insurance policy and interest).

♦ Next you need to contact the insurance company which issued the endowment policy and ask for a **surrender value** (i.e. the amount you would get if you cancelled the policy). When you have this figure seek independent financial advice – perhaps from the financial advisor you had when you took out the policy if you trust them.

♦ If the repayment mortgage monthly payments are less than the combined payments of interest and the endowment policy premiums, then it will probably be best to switch. Remember there will also be a lump sum from the cancellation of the insurance policy. Use this to help you with paying off the high priority debt repayments. You will have to show you have received the money from your policy in your personal budget.

♦ You will need some form of life insurance to pay off the mortgage if you die. Or you could get a mortgage protection policy to cover illness or unemployment. But think carefully about whether this type of insurance will really help and *shop around for the best deal.*

Extending the mortgage term

This will reduce the monthly payments. But of course you will pay more interest in total, because you are borrowing for longer. Consider extending the mortgage if you switch from endowment to repayment as this will reduce the payments even more.

Paying interest only

If you have a repayment mortgage, you could ask your lender to accept a monthly payment which covers only the interest part of the normal monthly payment. This may be acceptable to them if they think the causes of your problems are temporary (e.g. unemployment or short-term illness). The more recently the mortgage was taken out, the smaller the reduction in the size of the monthly payment an interest only deal will be, because in the early stages you are paying a higher proportion of the total payment as interest. But it could be a help.

Adding arrears to your mortgage

If the value of your home is more than the outstanding mortgage, the lender may agree to add your arrears to the total mortgage. The monthly payments will be increased or the mortgage period extended to take account of this. It's sometimes called **capitalising arrears**. Your lender is more likely to agree to this if you have already kept to a payment agreement for a reasonable period.

If you get a deal – stick to it!

Remember, the mortgage lender holds all the good cards. Somehow, you have to get them to trust you. Make sure you stick to any arrangement you are able to agree with the lender. If you don't, you will quickly lose their sympathy and they will start getting tough. If you can't keep to the deal because your circumstances have changed, explain this to them *before* you have to reduce or stop the agreed payments.

If you can keep the deal with the mortgage lender by stopping paying some low priority debt (credit card minimum payments, for example), then it is worth doing.

What if you can't reach a deal you can afford?

Is the house worth more than the outstanding mortgage?

If so you could sell your existing house and go to a smaller and/or cheaper one. You would need your lender's agreement to do this as they hold the house deeds. But if they think it will help them get their money back they will probably agree. Although this will help pay off some debt, some of the capital released will go in estate agent fees, legal fees and stamp duty.

Negative equity?

If you are in a negative equity situation, or house value

and outstanding mortgage are roughly equal, downsizing won't help. Bear in mind, too, that going into rented accommodation will only cost less per month than the mortgage payments if the rented place is a lot smaller or in a cheaper area than the present house or flat.

You may be eligible for council or social housing, particularly if you have children, disabilities or are ill. But to stand a chance of qualifying for this you have to be actually homeless – so this last resort can only help if the Court has granted the lender repossession of your home. And that is what we are trying to avoid!

Thinking of handing in the keys? Think again!
Don't think that by handing in the keys and walking away your troubles will be over. They won't. The lender will take possession of the house and sell it, probably at a lower price than you could get yourself. They will add on a lot of extra charges for doing that and go on pursuing you for any difference between the outstanding debt (including the extra charges) and the proceeds of the sale of the house. You will be worse off than if you had stayed in the house until the lender went to court asking for repossession. And you definitely won't qualify for council housing because you will have made *yourself* homeless. We deal with how to present the best possible case to the Court using your personal budget, and by doing so to hopefully hold on to the house, in Chapter 7.

Any other loans secured on your house?
If you are having trouble paying off any other loans which are secured on your home, you have got to give these almost as much priority as your main mortgage.

The first step, as always, is to talk to the lender. Unfortunately the sort of company offering second mortgages or secured loans is likely to be a lot less sympathetic and more hard nosed than a building society or even a mainstream bank.

Next, have you any equity in your house? Is it worth more than the outstanding *main* mortgage? If so, and if you are still up to date with your main mortgage repayments, then approach your main lender to ask if they will increase your main mortgage. This will almost certainly be at a lower interest rate than you are paying on the second mortgage or secured loan. You might at the same time consider extending the period of the first mortgage so as to reduce the new level of repayments closer to the amount you were originally paying on the first mortgage.

If your main lender agrees to lend you more, see if the second mortgage lender will agree to take a lump sum settlement of the loan without big penalties. If so, then go ahead with the increase in the first mortgage. If not, it may still be worth increasing the first mortgage, and using the money raised to pay off the arrears on the second mortgage. Put what is left in the highest secure interest account you can find and use the account to pay off the interest and capital instalments on the second mortgage or secured loan from this for the remainder of the period of the loan. You will have to be strong minded though and make absolutely sure you don't use it for anything else – unless you have to use it as part of an agreement with all outstanding creditors.

If you can't increase your first mortgage and you can't make any further cutbacks in other spending, then you've got to take the same steps as if you were in trouble with the first mortgage. Make the best offer you can afford and if the lender refuses it, you will have to make the best possible case in court with the use of your personal budget.

Second mortgage companies are less scrupulous than building societies and may use debt collectors to threaten you with eviction. Remember *no one* can evict you from any property without a Court Order.

WHAT ABOUT TENANTS RATHER THAN HOMEOWNERS?

What if you are in trouble with the rent rather than the mortgage?

The most important thing to remember is that whatever type of tenancy you hold, *no tenant can be evicted without a court order.*

There are various types of tenancy, the most common being shorthold assured tenancy which means that you can be asked to leave after the initial assured period (usually six months) has ended. Even with this type of tenancy, only a court order can allow legal eviction, although once the assured period of the shorthold tenancy is over and has not been renewed, a landlord need only demonstrate that they have given notice that the tenancy is ended to obtain a Court Order.

With all types of tenancy, though, failure to pay the rent can lead to a Court Order permitting eviction. It is therefore as important to pay the rent as to pay the mortgage.

If you get into rent arrears, talk to the landlord – they may be sympathetic. A Court, though, is more likely to grant a landlord possession for rent arrears, whatever the reasons for your difficulty in paying, than to grant a mortgage lender possession for mortgage arrears. So keep paying the rent.

What if you can't pay the rent?
Remember the following:

◆ Harassment, including threats, visits or phone calls at inappropriate times (such as late at night or at work) is a criminal offence. If it happens you should seek advice from an organisation like the Citizens Advice Bureaux.

- You may be entitled to Housing Benefit if your income falls below a certain level either temporarily, through illness or unemployment, or permanently. If you think there is any possibility of qualifying, contact the housing department of your local council.

- If you have become homeless through no fault of your own, your local council may have an obligation to re-house you. In order to stand any chance of being re-housed, you must have been evicted after a Court Order. It is important, therefore, if you can't pay the rent to go through Court Proceedings until you are evicted. If you give up the tenancy before this you will be seen by the housing department as having made yourself deliberately homeless and you will not qualify for re-housing.

- Advice on how to handle Court Proceedings for eviction is in Chapter 7.

COUNCIL TAX ARREARS

If you cannot pay Council Tax the council has some tough powers to get the money out of you. They can go to a Magistrates Court and get a Liability Order for the amount you owe. They can then force your employer to deduct the amount owing in instalments from your pay and send the money to them. They can get the bailiffs to call. They can apply to the County Court to put a 'charge' on your house (in other words the debt is secured on your house like a mortgage and so may put your house at risk). Finally, if all else fails they can apply to the Magistrates Court for an order for you to be sent to prison.

But don't panic! Prison really is a last resort and very rarely used. There are a lot of things you can do before things get that bad.

- Check whether you qualify for Council Tax Benefit. You could be if you are on a low income (temporarily or permanently) and have savings of less than £16,000, or are on Income Support or income based Job Seekers' Allowance.

- You may get a discount if you are the only adult in the house or the other adults are full-time students, on training schemes or have mental disability. There is also something called the Second Adult Rebate if you share the house with someone on a low income who does not pay rent and is not your spouse or partner.

- If none of these help and you cannot pay then contact the council and try to come to an arrangement using your personal budget to argue your case.

- Keep paying whatever you can afford even if it's less than you should be paying.

- Contact your local councillor and explain your difficulties to them. This will at least ensure you get a sympathetic hearing from the council and your councillor may be able to help you negotiate a rate of payment you can afford.

UTILITY BILLS

Gas and electricity
If you don't pay your electricity or gas bill, your supplier can

cut you off. They don't need a court order to do this, so you need to make payment of these bills a priority debt. If you are having problems, here are some suggestions:

- Talk to the supplier at the most senior level you can get to as soon as possible.

- Ask to pay your bills by weekly or monthly instalments or under a budget plan, where your bills over both winter and summer are averaged out. If you have arrears you can ask for this to be included in the budget plan. Use your personal budget as evidence of how much you can afford to pay.

- You could agree to a pre-payment meter if you have significant arrears. You pay for your current use of gas and/or electricity through a token, pre-payment card or coins. If there are arrears, the rate you pay for each unit is set at a higher level until the arrears are paid off. Make sure that you can afford the rate set to pay off arrears. Argue the case using your personal budget if it is set too high. The downside of this is that if you have no cash tokens or credit on your pre-payment card, you will get no gas or electricity.

- Ask for a book of payment slips and keep paying off as much as you can. As long as you are paying something they will be reluctant to cut you off.

- The supplier is unlikely to agree to settle for an amount of less than the cost of the fuel you are using plus a contribution to arrears. You may have to reduce your use of fuel to the absolute minimum. Put on an extra fleece and get out the torch!

- Most fuel companies will not disconnect you in winter if all the adults in the house are over retirement age or there is someone seriously ill living there.

- Contact the Social Services Department of your local council. The fuel company will delay cutting you off if Social Services or the Department of Work and Pensions are looking into your case – particularly if children are involved.

WATER

Water companies cannot cut off your water supply because you are in arrears with your water/sewerage rates. They will pursue the debt in the same way as credit card companies or other creditors where the debt is not secured on your house.

OTHER DEBTS

Hire purchase

Hire purchase agreements are different from credit agreements. Unlike credit agreements, you don't own the goods under a hire purchase agreement until you have paid the last instalment. If you fall into arrears and have not paid more than one third of the total owing, the hire purchase lender can repossess the goods without a Court Order. As the most frequently bought items under hire purchase agreements are cars, and they tend to be left around in the streets, it's quite easy for the HP companies to get their hands on them.

If you have paid more than one third of the amount owing and want to keep the goods (perhaps you need the car to get to work), you will need to attend Court, and offer the normal payments plus something towards the arrears. You could try offering something less than the normal payments, but you will need to use your personal budget to show this is all you can afford, and HP companies are unlikely to accept this. If you are in trouble with HP payments you need advice. Go to your Citizens Advice Bureau for help.

Owing money to your bank

If the bank where you have your current account is owed money on credit cards it has issued, or on unsecured personal loans or on overdrafts, life can get difficult. They will try to control your debt repayments to ensure they get paid first! This will not be in your best interest. If your salary or wage is paid directly into that account, the bank will have a nasty habit of taking out of your account anything it is owed, leaving you with nothing to pay the higher priority debts such as your mortgage.

The first step is to try to get an agreement with the bank on what you can afford to pay, using the good old personal budget statement. What sort of letter should you write to banks and other lenders, where the loan is *not* secured on your house? Keep it simple and to the point. There is no point in pleading. Just stick to the facts. Examples of what you might send are shown in Appendices A1–A4. If they don't respond favourably to this, you need to act quickly to stop them taking the new money being paid into your account from wages or salary. Open an account with a different bank or building society and ask your employer to pay wages or salary into the new account immediately. If necessary, explain the circum-stances to your employer so that there is no delay. Any bank you approach to open an account will carry out credit checks on you. They will discover you have problems and if they agree to open an account it will be a 'basic account'. This will provide the usual direct debit and standing order facilities, but will not issue a cheque book or allow an overdraft.

◆ You are then in a much stronger position to negotiate with the bank to which you owe the money. Ask them to stop adding interest and charges to the current account so that you have a chance of paying off the debt. They should see that you have a chance of paying off the debt. They should see that if they don't agree to stop adding interest and the money you pay them does not reduce the debt, you have no incentive to pay any more.

◆ If the staff at your local branch do not agree to this, contact the regional or head office of the bank.

◆ If you owe the bank a lot of money, they may ask you to agree to a 'voluntary' charge on your house in return for reduced payments. This could put your home at risk in the same way as mortgage arrears. *Do not agree to it without considering the implications very carefully or without obtaining legal advice.* If a voluntary charge is suggested, go to your local Citizens Advice Bureau for advice.

Debts to friends and relations
These can be very difficult. You naturally want to pay

them back as soon as possible so as not to damage friendships or family relationships. This can cause problems as your other creditors may claim that you are paying more on a personal debt than is 'fair'. You will have to explain this to the friend or relation to whom you owe money.

Child Support Payments

If you are liable to make Child Support Payments and stop paying them, the Child Support Agency can collect the payments which are due direct from your employer from your wages or salary.

If they can't get what they are due this way, they can apply to a Magistrates Court for a Liability Order. Once they have this they can:

♦ use bailiffs to seize goods and sell them to raise money

♦ get a charge on your property which puts your home at risk

♦ seize money from your bank account

♦ ask the Court to send you to prison!

Try to make an arrangement on payments and arrears to pay the CSA using your personal budget. They don't have a reputation for either efficiency or sympathy!

WHAT IF YOUR CREDITORS WON'T PLAY BALL?

Don't give up. If they take you to Court to get money out of you they need to have shown they have acted reasonably. By demonstrating you have done everything you can to pay, you put pressure on them to respond. Steps you should take:

◆ Start paying the amount you have offered.

◆ Write to the creditor again, asking them to reconsider your offer (see Appendix A2).

◆ If some other creditors have accepted your offer, point this out to creditors who haven't accepted.

◆ If they send someone round to try to persuade you to pay up, don't let them get you to pay more than you have offered. If you do, you won't have the money to pay creditors you've already made a deal with.

Heard of debt consolidation companies?

You may have seen adverts from companies promising to 'set you free from debt', 'save you up to 50% on your total debt repayments' and making other extravagant claims.

Be very careful. These offers are not all they seem and could land you in deeper trouble for the following reasons:

◆ The loan offered to replace unsecured loans will be secured on your home. By signing up you put your home at risk and are in a worse position than before.

◆ The interest rates shown on the adverts are the absolute minimum they charge. Usually these are only made to people with good credit records and with equity in their home. If you have these, you probably won't need a loan from a company like this. If you don't have, then you will be charged a much higher rate.

◆ Advertisements for the companies show a much lower rate of monthly repayment than the sum of existing credit card and personal loan repayments. This is usually because the period of the loan offered is much, much longer than the loans it is replacing. You will be paying a lot more interest over the longer period and there will usually be big penalty payments if you try to pay the loan off early.

◆ There may be set-up and administrative fees rolled into the loan which don't show up in the quoted APR.

Debt management companies

Debt management companies are different from debt consolidation companies. Instead of offering a loan, debt management companies offer to reach agreements with creditors and provide a channel for the money you can pay to your creditors. They charge a substantial fee for doing this – often one month's total repayments and then a percentage of subsequent payments as well. *You can get this service free through National Debtline.*

In general, the advice is don't get involved with debt management or debt consolidation companies.

Debt management companies should not be confused with the debt management plan offered by National Debtline (see page 116) – a charity that offers good advice on debt problems. Their Debt Management Plan applies to people with debts of over £5,000, more than three creditors and a minimum income of £100 per month. The Plan offers to work out what you can afford to pay each month, talks to your creditors and receives the money from you to pay out to creditors on the agreed basis. Get in touch with National Debtline if you think this would help.

What if creditors get nasty?

If you can't make a deal with creditors, they will try to put pressure on you. There are limits on what they can legally do. They are committing a **criminal** offence if they:

◆ phone you late at night or repeatedly at work

◆ park a van or car marked 'debt collector' outside your house

◆ contact your employer about your debt.

If a creditor does any of the above, contact the Citizens Advice Bureau or your local Council's Trading Standards Department.

A creditor might pass the debt on to a collection agency. *Don't worry.* They have no greater powers, and are bound by the same legal restrictions listed above as are the creditors.

The final step a creditor can take is through the Courts. Even if it comes to this, there is a lot you can do to protect your home and your vital possessions. That's in the next chapter.

7

If The Worst Comes to The Worst

So everything you have done so far to resolve your debt crisis has failed. The County Court papers start arriving. What now?

The first piece of advice is the best advice at all stages of debt problems: Don't panic!

There is no need to be frightened of the Courts. They are not there to punish you for debt. They are there to settle disputes about money owed and to decide how money that really is owed should be repaid. They are also there to protect you against unfair or unreasonable claims.

WHAT IS THE PROCEDURE?

◆ First you will receive a **Claim Form** from the Court. This will set out what your creditor believes you owe them – the **Particulars of the Claim.**

◆ You will either agree or disagree with the claim. You may disagree that there is a debt at all, or disagree with the amount of the debt.

◆ If you agree with the amount of the claim, you fill in the **Admission Form.** (A copy of this is shown in Appendix B1(ii).) Instructions on how to do this come with the Form. Your personal budget will help you do this as the Admission Form also asks for full details of income and essential outgoings. There is also a section to include the payments you are already making on your priority debts and any other Court Judgements you might have.

◆ The Admission Form also includes a section to make an offer of payment. It is vital you make an offer. The offer should be the most you can reasonably afford based on what you are telling the Court in your personal budget.

◆ You must send in the Admission Form within the time limit (16 days from the date of the postmark).

- *If you don't meet this deadline, the Court may order you to pay the whole amount owed at once.*

- If the creditor accepts your offer of payment, you will receive a Court Order to make payments to the creditor (not the Court) and keep a record of what you have paid.

- If the creditor does not accept your offer, the Court will determine what you should pay each month. This is done by post without you having to attend Court if the debt is less than £50,000.

- If you can't afford what the Court decides, you can ask the Court to look again – a **Redetermination**. You must ask for this within 14 days of getting the Court Order. You can ask for a Hearing on the Redetermination which you can attend in order to make your case in person. It usually takes place in the District Judge's private rooms rather than in open Court.

- If you get to the stage where Court Procedures are started with debt problems – go to your local Citizens Advice Bureau or Local Authority Debt Counselling Service for advice. They are experts at helping you fill in the forms for County Courts, and will reassure you about procedure.

- If your total debt is less than £5,000 you may be able to apply for an **Administration Order**. This is a way of putting all your debts together and making one monthly payment into Court. The Court then shares it out among your creditors on a basis the Court considers reasonable. Your creditors can't take any further action against you if you have an Administration Order. Obviously, it is vital you keep paying the amount agreed with the Court.

If you don't agree with the Claim or wish to make a Counter Claim

◆ Instead of filling in the Admission Form, you should fill in the **Defence Form** (Appendix B2) and send it back to the Court.

◆ You should only do this if you dispute the debt or the amount of the debt. If you dispute how much you can afford to pay, then you do this through filling in the Admission Form.

◆ Defending a claim against you for debt is complicated. You should seek advice through the Citizens Advice Bureau or Local Authority Debt Counselling Service who can get you access to a certain amount of free legal advice. You could contact the National Debtline (see page 117).

What if you can't or don't pay what the Court orders?

If you don't pay the monthly amount the Court orders the creditor will probably ask the Court to take further action. This could be one or more of the following:

◆ **Attachment of earnings**. The Court can order your employer to make deductions from your wages or salary to clear the debt. There is a set formula for working out how much can be recovered by this method.

◆ **Charging Order**. The debt becomes secured on your

home like your mortgage. This can put your home at risk. There must be a Court Hearing before a charging order can be made and you can argue against it at that hearing. You will need advice in these circumstances. Go to the Citizens Advice Bureau or similar organisation.

◆ **Bailiffs' Warrant**. The creditor can ask the Court to issue a Warrant of Execution from the County Court Bailiffs. If this happens, you can get the warrant suspended by filling a County Court Form 245 and making an offer of payment you can afford. Seek advice on this from the local Citizens Advice Bureau or Debt Counselling Service.

Two things to remember if the bailiffs come to call
1. They have no right to force entry to your house. Do not let them in under any circumstances and make sure every member of your household understands that they must not be let in.

2. Bailiffs cannot take basic household goods. They could, though, take a car belonging to you parked outside or nearby.

Being taken to Court is not the end of the world
Surprisingly, there are some advantages in being taken to Court.

◆ The Court will usually stop interest being charged on credit agreements under £5,000. If you owe more, the creditor can get the Court to allow them to charge interest.

- The Court is likely to let you pay a monthly amount which you can afford. This is why an accurate and realistic statement of income and essential outgoings is so important.

- The creditors should not harass you during the period the matter is in the hands of the Courts. If they do, report them to the Court.

But there is a downside!

- Court costs will be added to your debt.

- County Court Judgements (CCJs) are recorded on a register and passed to credit agencies. This will probably make it difficult for you to get credit in the future.

- If you don't pay the monthly amount ordered by the Court, further action will be taken (see above). It is vital to keep up the payments ordered by the Court if you possibly can.

SHOULD I, CAN I, GO BANKRUPT?

You will have heard of people going bankrupt in order to get free of their debts, particularly if they owe tens of thousands of pounds. Bankruptcy doesn't carry the stigma it once did. In certain circumstances it can even have advantages for the individual who is in debt. The government has brought in new legislation which helps people who go bankrupt if there has been no deliberate fraud or reckless behaviour. Under this legislation, debtors can be free of their debts only a year after being declared bankrupt.

There are advantages and disadvantages of making yourself bankrupt.

Advantages

- Once you are bankrupt your creditors can usually take no further action against you. For this reason, they are very unlikely to seek your bankruptcy unless you have substantial assets like a house.

- At the end of the period of bankruptcy, debts that have not been paid are **written off**, but you may be asked to enter a legal agreement to pay monthly instalments to the Official Receiver from your income for up to three years.

Disadvantages

- If you have significant assets, such as equity in your home, you will lose them if you are made bankrupt.

- During the period you are in bankruptcy – now generally a year – you are subject to many restrictions on spending and saving.

- You will find it difficult to get credit in the future.

- Making yourself bankrupt costs several hundred pounds in fees and so is unlikely to benefit you unless you have high debts, no assets and no prospect of paying off your debts.

If you think you may be made bankrupt, you should seek advice.

WHERE TO GET GOOD ADVICE ON DEBT FOR *FREE*

Throughout this book, the advice has been that however serious the problem seems to be – *don't panic*. One reason for not panicking is that there is a lot of free help and advice available. The important thing is to access that advice *as soon as possible* as the problems start to emerge. It is important to seek advice early for two reasons:

1. There is often a waiting list for free, detailed advice on debt so the sooner you get on the list the better.

2. The quicker you get advice and put it into practice, the easier the problems will be to solve.

Places to go for advice and help

Citizens Advice Bureaux (CABs) and Local Advice Centres
Most large towns and cities have either a Citizens Advice Bureau or an Independent Advice Centre. You will get a similar range of advice from either of these. To contact them look up in the *Yellow Pages* under Counselling and Advice. In this section you will find both Citizens Advice Bureaux and Local Advice Centres listed. *Avoid the private counsellors or private debt counselling companies you see listed. They are there to make money out of you rather than to help you.*

CABs and Local Advice Centres not only give advice themselves, they may also refer you to specialised services when you need those services. They will get you on the list for specialised free debt counselling. They will help you access half an hour of free legal advice including advice on whether you might be entitled to Legal Aid (now called help from the Community Legal Service Fund). Even if you don't qualify for more than the initial half hour of free legal advice, the Advice Centre will tell you which solicitors specialise in debt problems or any special type of problem you have. They may refer you to the local Trading Standards Department if your debts have arisen from dodgy traders or credit agreements.

The key thing they will do is to listen to your problem. They will try to sort it out there and then if that is possible (though it may not be in debt cases). They may contact creditors on your behalf, e.g. utility companies, to see if they can get the pressure taken off while a solution is found.

Some of the staff are full-time paid staff. Others are volunteers but all are very well trained and the standard of advice they give is high – frequently checked and audited by independent bodies. All provide absolute confidentiality about your affairs. Sometimes Advice Centres are provided by local authorities, particularly Advice Centres specialising in financial problems. These are also friendly, confidential and efficient.

Other sources of advice
There are also a number of charities specialising in offering advice on debt. Perhaps the best known of these is The National Debtline Service. It provides a National Telephone Helpline for people with debt problems. It also provides a range of very useful pamphlets and booklets on particular subjects, such as County Court Procedures, Bankruptcy and Harassment.

If you have difficulty in finding a nearby Citizens Advice
Bureau or other Advice Centre, contact:

> National Association of Citizens Advice Bureaux
> 115–123 Pentonville Road
> London N1 9LZ
> www.citizensadvice.org.uk

Or Advice UK
> 12th Floor
> London Bridge House
> 25 London Bridge Street
> London SE1 9ST
> Tel: 020 7407 4070
> www.adviceuk.org.uk

Or National Debtline
> The Arch
> 48–52 Floodgate Street
> Digbeth
> Birmingham B19 3RL
> Freephone helpline: 0808 8084000
> www.nationaldebtline.co.uk

Or Playpan
> Kempton House
> Dysart Road
> Grantham
> Lincolnshire NG31 7LE
> Tel: 0800 716239
> www.fcl.org.uk

Remember none of these organisations can solve your
problem for you. Only you can do that. But they can give

you guidance and reassurance about the best way to go about solving the problem.

HOW TO LIVE IN PEACE AND FREEDOM

Golden rules to give peace of mind and freedom to enjoy life:

♦ Never borrow to cover routine spending. Only borrow for a specific purpose – for example, house or car purchase, home improvements.

♦ When deciding how much you need and can afford, always allow a margin for unforeseen events – like a significant rise in interest rates, illness, or a reduction in bonus.

♦ Always shop around for the best *total* deal: interest rates are not the only factor to take into account. Look at up front admin/arrangement fees, compulsory insurance, whether early repayment is allowed.

♦ Always read the small print. This is where the rip-offs are hidden. Don't assume that because you are dealing with a big name bank or other financial institution they won't try to rip you off. Remember banks have made huge profits in recent years and they don't make these profits by great management skill. They make them by ripping off their customers!

♦ If problems arise, don't ignore them. They won't go away and the longer you leave them, the worse they get.

♦ Don't borrow more money to pay off existing debts without thinking hard about the consequences –

particularly if the new loan is secured on your home.

◆ If you are facing financial problems always check that you are claiming all the benefits and tax credits you are entitled to.

◆ If you can't meet debt repayments, contact your creditors straight away to explain your difficulties. Write, phone or if they have a local branch, go and see them.

◆ Don't get involved with debt management companies. They will probably make matters worse.

◆ Make sure you tackle your priority debts first – particularly those where non-payment could mean the loss of your home: mortgage, rent, secured personal loans.

◆ Seek advice at the earliest possible time from organisations like the Citizens Advice Bureaux or National Debtline. Remember a lot of people have debt problems, and you may have to wait for detailed expert advice, so get in the queue.

◆ If your creditors take you to Court, make sure you reply to Court Papers within the time limit.

◆ If you reach agreement on repayment with your creditors or the Court makes a payment order, you must stick to it. If your circumstances change for the worse, go back to your creditors or the Court and explain why you can no longer pay what was agreed.

◆ Keep copies of all letters to and from creditors and the Court.

Appendices

EXAMPLE LETTERS TO CREDITORS

Appendix A1
Letter to creditor informing them that you are unable to make monthly payments (e.g. credit card, personal loan).

Your address

Reference or customer number if appropriate

Date

Creditor's address

Dear Sir/Madam

A/c No 12345

I am unable to meet the (minimum) monthly payment on the above account. This is because (give reason unemployment, ill health, etc). I hope that my circumstances will improve and enable me to make full payment at some time in the future. In the meantime, however, I am in a position to make a payment of only £   per month. I enclose a personal budget sheet which shows my total income from all sources and my total outgoings. As you can see, I have only £   for my creditors. The payments

I am proposing to pay to other creditors are made on a pro rata basis, i.e. on the basis of the same percentage of the debt.

In view of my present circumstances, would you please accept the above offer. If interest or other charges are being added to the account, I would be grateful if you would freeze these so that all the payments I make will reduce what I owe you.

Should my circumstances improve, I will contact you again with a view to increasing the payments I make to you.

I would be grateful if you would send a payment book/ standing order/direct debit form to make it easier to pay you.

I look forward to hearing from you as soon as possible.

Yours faithfully

Signature

Your name – PRINTED

Appendix A2

Letter to creditor who refuses an offer of payment

Your address

Reference or customer number if appropriate

Date

Creditor's address

Dear Sir/Madam

A/c No 12345

Thank you for your letter/phone call concerning the above account.

I am sorry you are unable to accept the offer which I have made. The majority of my creditors have accepted the offers made to them and I have commenced payments. I cannot offer you more because, as demonstrated by the personal budget sheet I sent you, I can only afford £ per month between all my creditors. If I pay you more, I have to breach the agreements I have made with other creditors. The offer made to you is on a pro rata basis, as used by the County Court.

On the basis of the above, I would be grateful if you would reconsider my offer. In order to demonstrate my good intent, I am starting to make the payments offered to your company on a weekly/monthly basis in order to reduce the debt to you.

I look forward to hearing from you as soon as possible.

Yours faithfully

Signature

Your name – **PRINTED**

Appendix A3

Letter to creditors informing them that you are not in a position to pay what had been previously agreed with them and are seeking to reduce payments to all creditors on a pro rata basis.

Your address

Reference or customer number if appropriate

Date

Creditor's address

Dear Sir/Madam

A/c No 12345

Since making an agreement with you on a reduced payment on the above account, I regret to say that my circumstances have changed. I can no longer afford the agreed monthly payments because ————

I enclose a revised personal budget sheet which shows my total income from all sources and my total outgoings. As you can see, there is only £   per month left for all my creditors.

The offers of reduced payments I have made to my creditors have been worked out on a pro rata basis and I have written to all creditors asking them to accept reduced payments on the same percentage basis.

In view of my circumstances, please would you accept a

reduced offer of £   per month. If interest or other charges are being added to the account, I would be grateful if you would freeze these so that all the payments I make will reduce what is owed to you.

Should my circumstances change, I will contact you again.

Thank you for your assistance. I look forward to hearing from you as soon as possible.

Yours faithfully

    Signature

Your name – PRINTED

Appendix A4

Letter to creditors informing them that your circumstances have changed and you are not in a position to make any payments or only token payments to any creditor.

Your address

Reference or customer number if appropriate

Date

Creditor's address

Dear Sir/Madam

A/c No 12345

Since making an agreement with you my circumstances have changed. I can now not afford to make the payments to you which we previously agreed. This is because

—————

I enclose a revised personal budget sheet which shows my total income from all sources and my total outgoings. As you can see, I have no money left over to make offers of payments to any of my creditors.

In these circumstances, would you please accept either suspension of all payments or a token payment of £1 per month with a review of the position in six months. If interest or other charges are being added to the account, I would be grateful if you would freeze these so my debt does not increase.

Should my circumstances improve, I will contact you immediately.

Thank you for your assistance. I look forward to hearing from you as soon as possible.

Yours faithfully

Signature

Your name – PRINTED

INTEREST PAYMENTS

Appendix A5

Differences in interest rates and the period of a loan make very big differences in the size of monthly payments and the total amount of interest paid over the life of the loan. Thus, if you agree to extend the life of the loan, the monthly payments will be lower. This appears to make loan consolidation offers very attractive. But the total interest paid over the life of the loan becomes very much larger even if the interest rate stays the same. Often companies offering debt management or loan consolidation charge a higher rate of interest as well as extending the period of the loan.

Here are some examples:

Size of loan	Period of loan	APR	Monthly payment	Total interest paid over period of loan	Total repayment (capital and interest)
£	years	%	£	£	£
10,000	5	7	198	1,880	11,880
10,000	25	7	70	11,203	21,203
10,000	10	6	111	3,322	13,322
10,000	10	9	126	5,201	15,201
25,000	5	8	506	5,415	30,415
25,000	20	8	209	25,186	50,186
25,000	20	12	275	41,065	66,065
100,000	5	11	2,174	30,454	130,454
100,000	25	11	980	194,034	294,034
100,000	25	6	644	93,290	193,290
100,000	25	9	839	151,758	251,758
250,000	30	6	1,498	289,595	539,595
250,000	30	9	2,011	474,160	724,160

Appendix B1 (i)

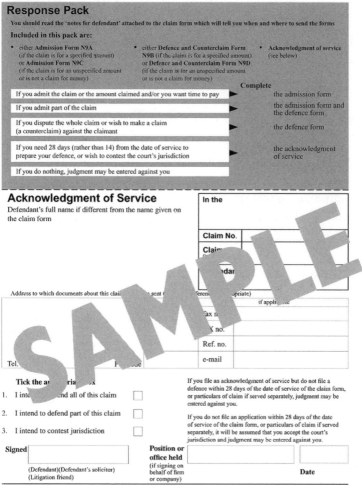

Response Pack

You should read the 'notes for defendant' attached to the claim form which will tell you when and where to send the forms

Included in this pack are:

- either **Admission Form N9A** (if the claim is for a specified amount) or **Admission Form N9C** (if the claim is for an unspecified amount or is not a claim for money)

- either **Defence and Counterclaim Form N9B** (if the claim is for a specified amount) or **Defence and Counterclaim Form N9D** (if the claim is for an unspecified amount or is not a claim for money)

- **Acknowledgment of service** (see below)

Complete

If you admit the claim or the amount claimed and/or you want time to pay	► the admission form
If you admit part of the claim	► the admission form and the defence form
If you dispute the whole claim or wish to make a claim (a counterclaim) against the claimant	► the defence form
If you need 28 days (rather than 14) from the date of service to prepare your defence, or wish to contest the court's jurisdiction	► the acknowledgment of service
If you do nothing, judgment may be entered against you	

Acknowledgment of Service

Defendant's full name if different from the name given on the claim form

In the

Claim No.

Clai~

~dar

Address to which documents about this clai~ ~ sent (~eren~ ~priate)

~ if appli~ ~

~ax n~

~ no.

Ref. no.

e-mail

Tel. ~ ~ue

Tick the a~ ~ria~ ~x

1. I inte~ ~nd all of this claim ☐

2. I intend to defend part of this claim ☐

3. I intend to contest jurisdiction ☐

If you file an acknowledgment of service but do not file a defence within 28 days of the date of service of the claim form, or particulars of claim if served separately, judgment may be entered against you.

If you do not file an application within 28 days of the date of service of the claim form, or particulars of claim if served separately, it will be assumed that you accept the court's jurisdiction and judgment may be entered against you.

Signed

(Defendant)(Defendant's solicitor) (Litigation friend)

Position or office held (if signing on behalf of firm or company)

Date

The court office at

is open between 10 am and 4 pm Monday to Friday. When corresponding with the court, please address forms or letters to the Court Manager and quote the claim number.

N9 Response Pack (5.02)

Printed on behalf of The Court Service

Appendix B1 (ii)

Admission (unspecified amount, non-money and return of goods claims)	In the	
	Claim No.	
	Claimant (including ref.)	
	Defendant	

- Before completing this form please read the notes for guidance attached to the claim form. If necessary provide details on a separate sheet, add the claim number and attach it to this form.
- If you are not an individual, you should ensure that you provide sufficient details about the assets and liabilities of your firm, company or corporation to support any offer of payment made.

In non-money claims only

☐ I admit liability for the whole claim
(Complete section 11)

In return of goods cases only

Are the goods still in your possession?
☐ Yes ☐ No

Part A Response to claim (tick one box only)

☐ I admit liability for the whole claim but want the court to decide the amount I should pay / value of the goods

OR

☐ I admit liability for the claim and offer to
pay [ ] in satisfaction of the claim
(Complete part B and sections 1-11)

Part B How are you going to pay the amount you have admitted? (tick one box only)

☐ I offer to pay on (date) [ ]

OR

☐ I cannot pay the amount immediately ~~...~~

[ ]

~~...~~ ffer to pay by ins ~~...~~ s of [ ]
~~...~~ k)(month)

1 Personal d ~~...~~

Surn: [ ]

Forename [ ]

☐ Mr ☐ Mrs ☐ Miss ☐ Ms

☐ Married ☐ Single ☐ Other (specify) [ ]

Age [ ]

Address [ ]
Postcode [ ]
Tel. no. [ ]

2 Dependants (people you look after financially)

Number of children in each age group

under 11 [ ] 11-15 [ ] 16-17 [ ] 18 & over [ ]

Other dependants [ ]
(give details)

3 Employment

☐ I am employed as a [ ]
My employer is [ ]

Jobs other than
main job (~~...~~ d~~...~~ ify)

☐ I ~~... em~~ ~~...~~ s a ~~...~~
~~...~~ rno ~~...~~ £ [ ]

☐ ~~...~~ rrears wit ~~...~~ rance
~~...~~ ions, income tax

☐ I ~~...~~ rears and I owe.......... £ [ ]

~~...~~ e de ~~...~~
ontracts and
other work in hand
(b) any sums due
for work done [ ]

☐ I have been unemployed for [ ] years [ ] months

☐ I am a pensioner

4 Bank account and savings

☐ I have a bank account
  ☐ The account is in credit by....... £ [ ]
  ☐ The account is overdrawn by.... £ [ ]

☐ I have a savings or building society account
  The amount in the account is......... £ [ ]

5 Residence
I live in ☐ my own property ☐ lodgings
  ☐ jointly owned house ☐ rented property
  ☐ council accommodation

N9C - w5 Admission (unspecified amount and non-money claims) (8.99)   *Printed on behalf of The Court Service*

Appendix B2(i)

Defence and Counterclaim
(unspecified amount, non-money and
return of goods claims)

- Fill in this form if you wish to dispute all or part of the claim and/or make a claim against the claimant (a counterclaim)
- You have a limited number of days to complete and return this form to the court.
- Before completing this form, please read the notes for guidance attached to the claim form.
- Please ensure that all the boxes at the top right of this form are completed. You can obtain the correct names and number from the claim form. The court cannot trace your case without this information.

How to fill in this form
- Set out your defence in section 1. If necessary continue on a separate piece of paper making sure that the claim number is clearly shown on it. In your defence you must state which allegations in the particulars of claim you deny and your reasons for doing so. **If you fail to deny an allegation it may be taken that you admit it.**
- If you dispute only some of the allegations you must
  - specify which you admit and which you deny; and
  - give your own version of events if different from the claimant's.

In the	
Claim No.	
Claimant (including ref.)	
Defendant	

- If the claim is for money and you dispute the claimant's statement of value, you must say why and if possible give your own statement of value.
- If you wish to make a claim against the claimant (a counterclaim) complete section 2.
- Complete and sign section 3 before returning this form.

Where to send this form
- send or take this form immediately to the court at the address given on the claim form.
- Keep a copy of the claim form and the defence form.

Community Legal Service Fund (CLSF)
You may qualify for assistance from the CLSF (this used to be called 'legal aid') to meet some or all of your legal costs. Ask about the CLSF at any county court office or any information or help point which displays this logo.

1. Defence

SAMPLE

Appendix B2(ii)

Defence and Counterclaim (specified amount)	**In the**	
	Claim No.	
	Claimant (including ref.)	
	Defendant	

Defence and Counterclaim (specified amount)

- Fill in this form if you wish to dispute all or part of the claim and/or make a claim against the claimant (counterclaim).
- You have a limited number of days to complete and return this form to the court.
- Before completing this form, please read the notes for guidance attached to the claim form.
- Please ensure that all boxes at the top right of this form are completed. You can obtain the correct names and number from the claim form. The court cannot trace your case without this information.

How to fill in this form

- Complete sections 1 and 2. Tick the correct boxes and give the other details asked for.
- Set out your defence in section 3. If necessary continue on a separate piece of paper making sure that the claim number is clearly shown on it. In your defence you must state which allegations in the particulars of claim you deny and your reasons for doing so. **If you fail to deny an allegation it may be taken that you admit it.**
- If you dispute only some of the allegations you must
  - specify which you admit and which you deny; and
  - give your own version of events if different from the claimant's.

- If you wish to make a claim against the claimant (a counterclaim) complete section 4.
- Complete and sign section 5 before sending this form to the court. Keep a copy of the claim form and this form.

Community Legal Service Fund (CLSF)

You may qualify for assistance from the CLSF (this used to be called 'legal aid') to meet some or all of your legal costs. Ask about the CLSF at any county court office or any information or help point which displays this logo.

1. How much of the claim do you dispute?

☐ I dispute the full amount claimed as shown on the claim form

or

☐ I admit the amount of £ _____

If you dispute only part of the claim you must **either:**

- pay the amount admitted to the person named at the address for payment on the claim form (see How to Pay in the notes on the back of, or attached to, the claim form). Then send this defence to the cou...

or

- complete the admission ... **and** this ... and send them to the ...

☐ I paid the amoun... ...(date)...

... the co... ... ...mission... ...2)

2. Do you dispute this claim because yo...
have already paid it? Tick whichever appli...

☐ No (go to section 3)

☐ Yes ... ... to the clai...
... ...m was issued)

... det... ...ow yo... ...
...y (the...

3.

Index

accident insurance, 57
administration charges, 35,
  37, 42, 118
annuity payments, 81
assured shorthold tenancy,
  28, 96
attachment of earnings, 31,
  111

bailiffs, 34, 35, 72, 90, 98,
  104, 112
bankruptcy, 113–114, 116
banks, 22, 23, 28, 30, 34,
  37, 39, 42, 59, 61–63, 77,
  82, 87, 95, 102–103, 118
base rate, 38, 50
budget (personal/
  household), 24, 30, 78–
  88, 96, 99, 100, 109
building society, 2, 3, 6, 10,
  19, 23, 34, 39, 42, 46, 95,
  96

childminding costs, 9, 10,
  12, 17, 19, 79, 84

Child Support Agency, 104
Children's Tax Credit, 27,
  80, 119
Citizens' Advice Bureau,
  30, 70, 80, 91, 97, 102,
  103, 107, 110–112, 115–
  117, 119
commission, 44
Council Tax, 18, 24, 29, 84,
  89, 98
  Benefit, 99
  Rebate, 24, 99
County Court proceedings,
  31–35, 83, 86, 90, 91, 94,
  98, 104, 107, 108–113,
  119
  Administration Order,
    110
  Admission Form, 109,
    130
  Charging Order, 98, 111
  Claim Form, 109
  Court Order, 96, 98, 101
  Defence Form, 111, 131,
    132